"*Passion for the Inne[r city...]* entering into life with [...] humour, grace, mercy a[nd ...]. [...] as a pastor and inner-city dweller I was sucked in, churned around, disturbed by the spirit, moved by the story, changed by its grace and inspired by its courage to *exist with* and *suffer with*. Theologically it asks profound questions of the church and our lives."

Revd Dr Deirdre Brower Latz, Principal and Senior Lecturer in Pastoral and Social Theology, Nazarene Theological College

"Challenging and deeply relevant given all we face today with race, justice, poverty and what Christian faith has to offer. It's a strange comfort to know that others have gone before us and learnt hard won lessons for change. Indeed, insights here could not only help inspire a new generation to take up the call for radical discipleship and community building, but sustain them for the required decades needed for transformation. This is a must read for any would-be Christian disciples, justice activists and/or new monastics."

Rev Dr Ash Barker, author/speaker/activist, leader of Seedbeds

"Austin Smith's humble, slow story of co-existing in the joy and pain of inner city life whispers quietly into our attention-grabbing disembodied world and reminds us of another way. It's a costly way but it's the way of Christ. Anyone considering investing their lives anywhere would do well to read this first."

Andy Flannagan, Director of Christians in Politics; Author, *Those Who Show Up*

"It is now commonplace in Christian social ethics to talk about the need to 'be with' rather than 'doing for' or 'to' our neighbours. This book, published forty years ago and now re-published, offers an early articulation of exactly this Christian social ethic for our times. Austin Smith's extraordinary writing and his lived witness prefigures much of our current desire to move to modes of place-based accompaniment, mutual common life and radical social friendship. The re-publication of these reflections offers us a chance to think again about a generation whose stories we are at risk of losing in exactly the moment when we most need to pause and to hear, reflect and be inspired by them."

Dr Anna Rowlands, St Hilda Professor of Catholic Social Thought and Practice; Author, *Towards a Politics of Communion: Catholic Social Teaching in Dark Times*

Passion for the Inner City

1983

Passion for the Inner City

Transporting Monastic Life to
1970s Liverpool

Austin Smith

Published by LAB / ORA Press
A working name for Passionists in England and Wales

St. Peter's Community Centre
Charles Street
Coventry
CV1 5NP
United Kingdom

Second edition published 2022
Edited by Christopher Donald

First published in the UK in 1983 by Sheed & Ward Ltd

Copyright © 1983 by Austin Smith
Copyright © 2022 by Passionists in England & Wales

The right of Austin Smith to be identified as the Author
of this work has been asserted in accordance with the
Copyright, Designs and Patents Act 1988

Cover design: Alice Marwick

ISBN: 978-1-7397162-0-2
Ebook ISBN: 978-1-7397162-1-9

Printed and bound in the United Kingdom by IngramSpark

Contents

	Foreword	7
1	Nineteen Seventy-One	11
2	Searching for a new monasticism	22
3	Losing our assumptions	39
4	Rediscovering reflection	49
5	Losing the 'institutional mind'	61
6	Rediscovering humanity	73
7	Losing our sense of accomplishment	82
8	Facing the realities of powerlessness	95
9	Losing our dependencies	118
10	The realities of a new community	129
	Appendix: the priest-workers of France	151
	Bibliography	167

Foreword

Father Austin came to our community in 1971: over fifty years ago. The community we are talking about is 'inner-city' Liverpool 8, the home of the oldest black community in Europe. A community demonised by the media, police and institutions in the City and beyond. A community oppressed by poverty, economic crisis, systemic racism and community politics: the type of politics Father Austin was deeply passionate about.

There is an old Civil Rights saying that we abide by in our community: *"Nothing about us, without us, is for us."* Father Austin came to our community with no agenda or plan. He had a passion for humanity, for people and their survival, and totally immersed himself into our community. He just believed it was crucial to be in the actual physical conditions of inner-city life to understand what it was like. He knew you cannot help people if you do not know them. He became one of our community members and truly embraced us.

PASSION FOR THE INNER CITY

It was Father Austin's destiny that he, representing his faith, came to our community at a time when the faith of many was being tested in ways no-one could imagine. Ten years after Austin moved into Liverpool 8, our community went through events that hit international headlines: turbulent times known by the media as the 1981 Toxteth Riots. The systemic racism and oppression of the Liverpool 8 community came to a head, resulting in what we called uprisings. In the midst of it, Austin became one of our trusted friends, activists and advocates.

He lived and suffered with us. On a few occasions, individuals in our community—who did not know him—questioned his motives, and he was deeply hurt, as were we. On one occasion, he was told he should not be party to the discussions and action in relation to our black community; labelled 'a white liberal: the most dangerous person in the room'. I can tell you, as did those who vehemently defended him: he was not.

As he recounts that memory here, it's clear it caused him to question himself, although he worked through it, and kept going. In fact, he had earned his right to be there in our community, and all those instrumental meetings. Communities have many detractors and disrupters: Father Austin was not one of them. True blessings are few and far between, and we must embrace them when we receive them; Father Austin, for his part, truly embraced and was embraced by us. We are all activists: of God, of faith, of life, of social justice, of equality, of humanity.

Father Austin, along with others, helped secure the funding and the underwriting of the authorities to see a

8

fully-resourced Liverpool 8 Law Centre established in the heart of the community. It is the UK's first Black-established and Black-led law centre. He believed that we, as Liverpool Blacks, should be empowered to protect ourselves and our community in all matters relating to criminal justice, police violence and brutality; to have the confidence and resources to be able to effectively represent ourselves in all matters legal.

It was the strength of his investment in the idea that mobilised us to make that dream an achievable probability. There are memories of him sitting in the Charles Wootton basement, after the 1981 uprisings, negotiating with churches to fund the Liverpool 8 Law Centre. It is also highly likely that Father Austin's standing as a respected priest gave confidence to the institutions in funding this notion. They would never have trusted or allowed the Black community to do this alone, as ingrained institutional racism has seen this community marginalised and oppressed for many years.

Yet it was us in the Black community and our heritage that Father Austin learned from, and he was guided by. In the 80's, as a local man recalled to me, many young black kids were suspicious of what we considered back then to be the interference of white outsiders. They had been the bearers of so many of our original troubles that we were rightly suspicious. However, Father Austin was our friend: he was able to not only become one of the most trusted, respected and well-loved members of our community, devoted to championing equality, kindness and justice; he was also able to share common interests and understanding of us as young people. There are few who can do that.

PASSION FOR THE INNER CITY

One of Austin's conclusions in this book, as he tried to pull together the lessons of his inner-city life, is that the ruins of the past—whether once-great abbeys, or modern-day factories—grew from a lack of genuine reflection. He asks the question, to his own people: how many in the powerful Catholic Church were reflective and self-aware enough to see the legacy they were creating in communities like ours: terraced houses turned into slums; dock cranes lying idle; young people without hope; the horrors of slavery and racism embedded into the fabric of the City, in its very street names?

Today, this question is still relevant. As we make decisions and plans in the here and now, how prepared are we to truly reflect on the legacy we are leaving for the future generation?

— *Sonia Bassey MBE*

1

Nineteen Seventy-One

*A mission begins ~ From the monastery to
Liverpool ~ To exist with, and suffer with*

On 11 October 1971, I took up residence at Flat 3, 7 Ducie
Street, Liverpool 8. It was a one-bedroom flat on the first
floor of a 'converted' terrace house. The inner city is full of
such houses. They once belonged to established families.
When the families moved away, conscious of the gathering
twilight of the urban scene, landlords then took the houses
and rented them out to other families who were willing to
put up with outside toilets and general decay. Eventually,
voluntary or statutory housing agencies moved in, either to
renovate the property for family occupation or 'convert' the
houses into flats.

I seem to remember that house more by smell than
anything else. The house was permeated by a smell which
seemed to send out the message that nobody was going to
stay here very long. I was soon to become expert at identifying
the smell of the flat: it was the smell of mice. As it turned
out, it was not a case of one or two mice, but legions of
them. They found their way into cornflake packets and they
even found their way into an electric toaster. They crawled
out of the former with an understandable flatulence; the
latter, they sprang out of when it was switched on.

There were six residents in that house besides myself. Two widowed ladies lived in the two ground floor flats; an elderly married couple lived on the same landing as our flat; and an old gentleman, suffering from acute asthma, lived in the attic flat. For them, it was cheap enough accommodation, and they were there more because there was no place to go, rather than by personal commitment. I was there because I had freely decided to be there. I had left the monastery, left the pattern of priesthood I knew, and stepped into a new mode of life.

Even that first day, there were events that troubled me. In the process of house-hunting for this place, I was advised to visit an agency in the city. Whilst I was waiting, I sat next to a young mother with three small children. She was a 'one parent family', not by choice, but because it had turned out that way. She had no place to go that night, and only six pounds in her purse. She neither begged from me nor complained; but I thought then that it was not money or even houses which divided us. We were aliens to each other by reason of the constriction and openness of choices which we both had in life. The 'housing' condition of both of us was but a symbol of the poverty and the richness of our respective choices in life: it was *the power to choose* which divided us. The fact of the matter was, there was not the slightest possibility in life that I should ever be that way: the potential for powerlessness was not there, never mind the actuality. I knew this. I might rationalise it, but in the end I had to admit that insecurity would never touch me.

The first night, though, I pushed these troubling thoughts aside. My fellow Passionist Nicholas and myself

NINETEEN SEVENTY-ONE

had chosen the flat. I moved in on my own that night, to get things ready for the official start of the Mission. I admit to a certain kind of adventure and excitement. For a number of reasons, I want to quote in full the passage I wrote that night logging my entrance:

> At 11.35 p.m. on Monday, 11 October I took up residence at Flat 3, 7 Ducie Street, Liverpool 8. It has been a day of final preparation. It would be quite false for me to say that I was not emotionally moved. As I write these words at 11.45 I pray God that this venture will open another era in the life of the Passionists. I do not see this as a departure from the past, rather one sees it as part of a fulfilment. The past is not preserved in being repeated, it is only preserved by being transformed. If it is merely repeated or talked about, it becomes no more than a legend, but if it is transformed it gathers power for the future. I am hardly in the character of pioneering saints, my own personal life bears few marks of sanctity. I do no more than ask our founders, Paul of the Cross and Dominic Barberi, to intercede for myself and Nicholas soon to join me, that we may be instruments of his grace. I am conscious of all I owe to the Congregation which has educated, fed and clothed me, all that I have.

There are times in life when we look back upon what we have written or spoken and feel a shiver up the spine. When I reread these lines eleven years later I am not without embarrassment. They were not well-thought out sentences; they were an expression of feeling. I could feel myself standing, if you will, in two streams: one stream was that of my whole traditional religious life and priesthood; the other stream was being potentially open to richness of life, puzzlement in life, and, though it is difficult to express, tensions in life.

There is not the slightest doubt that the actual living conditions—that flat, those other occupants, and the actual physical environment—were key issues. My love for my religious life and priesthood were very real; but very real, too, was that physical living situation. It would be false to suggest that this living situation did not make a difference, that it was not in any way crucial. Of course it was. I felt exposed in a way in which I had never felt exposed before. It exposed me to the wonder and the tragedy of 'humanness' or 'being human'. It is an exposure which has ever evolved.

From the monastery to Liverpool

I was professed a Passionist on 15th December 1946, and ordained a priest in the same order on 27th February 1954. I in no way regret either event. On the contrary, I thank God and everyone who has been part of my making those decisions—and sustaining me in them through a period of thirty five years. However, it goes without saying that I, with so many other priests and religious who committed themselves to a particular mode of life so long ago, have been part of a changing religious life and priesthood. These last ten years especially have revolutionised my priestly and religious life.

Further still, these last ten years impel me to ask further questions. I ask them with all gentleness. Have priesthood and religious life faced the real issues in the sphere of radical renewal? Are we asking the right questions today? Although this question is addressed to priesthood and religious life, I hope to show that it has deep significance for the Church as a whole in its search for radicalisation, in the positive sense.

The Passionist inner city Mission in Liverpool was not an overnight creation. It was the result of years of discussion. Its seed is to be found in the General Chapter Document* of 1970:

> An increasingly important area of the apostolate is the work that must be undertaken for the de-Christianised groups or regions to make them once again living members of the Christian community. This apostolate will demand a deep sense of understanding that God may open to us a door for the word, to declare the mystery of Christ.

There were many at the Chapter of 1968-1970 who simply believed there was something else to be explored beyond the usual categorisation of the Congregation's work. More, I think that many of those religious† also believed that this commitment, no matter how vague, had something to do with the question of the poor.

Two things were certain. The Chapter was concerned with our so-called 'developed world'; and they were not

---

* The written report from a 'General Chapter', ie. the time where the members of a monastic Order meet together to discuss vision and direction.

† 'Religious' as a noun, a priest from a religious order.

considering anything that could fit into past patterns of thought or action.

A working party was set up to keep exploring the question; a little later, that somewhat vague commitment was refined by the working party's report, in these words:

> Given the courage, we could send a small team ... to live in one of our great conurbations and search for ways and means to bring Christ to them. Such a team would be without pastoral commitments in the sense of having a parish... What the details of that work would be cannot in the nature of the case be determined in advance.
>
> Much will depend on the location of the Mission, the actual and social problems met with... It will be a long task of searching for ways and means but it is here that the zeal, imagination and mutual consultation of the missionaries and that ingenious love of God of which our founder spoke, must be given full rein.

This was the basis on which I found myelf, in October 1971, settling into an area which had been specifically chosen for being categorised as an urban social malaise area. Our Order was fired with enthusiasm, yet as I woke each morning to a new structureless existence I did not find myself preoccupied with the missionary methodology of those reports. There were only three realities in my life. There was my faith, and with that faith my whole Passionist heritage; there was the vast population which swarmed around me; and I came to depend on another religious brother as I have never depended upon another fellow religious before.

I was without parish, without mission to be preached, or retreat to be given, without acceptability as a priest and religious in the ordinary way; I was without a defined life as I had known it in the past, or any kind of described way forward into the future.

I knew things would not be the same in my own life again, but never did I anticipate at that stage the revolution which must take place in myself. I was certainly conscious that I must do something for the inner city, but the thought gradually ate its way into my consciousness that the inner city was about to demand a revolution in me. It was not so much a question of rejecting a theology, but being forced to rethink it: the theology of 'existing with', and 'suffering with', those around me.

To exist with, and suffer with

One of my early loves in the world of philosophy was Maritain. Years ago he seemed to be asking questions which were so fundamental to life, and in recent days I have been re-reading his work. It has not been idle reading. He has been one of many authors I have gone to for help in an effort to reflect upon my life in the inner city. He has not offered me solutions or hard certitudes, but one passage has assisted me in attempting to formulate or clarify the issues which I will attempt to describe in these pages: issues about the church and the human, the loss of asceticism, and the real issues which priesthood and the religious life must face for radicalisation.

The passage seminally articulates what I wish to say about my experience in the inner city of Liverpool. I quote the passage in full:

> Whenever we have to deal with the ingredients of human history, we are prone to consider matters from the point of view of action or of ideas which shape action. Yet it is necessary to consider them also—and primarily—from the point of view of existence. I mean there is another, and more fundamental, order than that of social and political action; it is the order of communion in life, desire and suffering. In other words there must be recognised ... the category *to exist with and suffer with* ...
>
> To *act for* belongs to the realm of benevolence. To exist with and to suffer with, to the realms of love in unity. Love is given to an existing, concrete being ... The one I love, I love him right or wrong; and I wish to exist and suffer with him.
>
> To *exist with* is an ethical category. It does not mean to live with someone in a physical sense, or in the same way as he does; and it does not mean loving someone in the sense of wishing him well; it means loving someone in the sense of becoming one with him, of bearing his burdens, of living a common moral life with him, of feeling with him and suffering with him.
>
> If one loves that human thing which is called 'the people' and which, like all human and living things is, I know, very difficult to define, but all the more real, then one's first and basic wish will be to exist, to stay in communion with the people.
>
> Before doing them good, or working for their good, before following or rejecting the political line of this or that group, which claims to be supporting their interests, before weighing conscientiously the good and evil to be expected from the

NINETEEN SEVENTY-ONE

> doctrines and historical trends which ask for their support
> and choosing amongst them, or in certain exceptional cases,
> rejecting them all, before doing any of these things, one will
> have chosen to exist with the people, to suffer with the people,
> to assume the people's hardships and destiny.[1]

My coming to the inner city forced me into a state of immobility. The whole idea of activity, apostolic activity, had to be rethought in my own life; my life itself had to change. When the normal structural and institutional contexts for action were taken away from me, the result was not simply frustration—that is far too negative; I was forced into a reflection, from which emerged the understanding of 'existence with and suffering with' this world in which I found myself.

The consequences of this were, in my own terms, a period of deep spiritual refreshment. To truly 'see' anything, one must allow oneself both time and space to do so. One must stand within the presence of the object to be seen, one must share the space of that which one attempts to see. Time and space are intimately interwoven with the act 'to exist with and suffer with'. I believe the enrichment in my life came from the astonishment which took it over. I saw anew the sacredness of life and the revelation of God in the lives of those with whom I was privileged to exist, and attempted— for attempt it can only be—to suffer.

All prayer and examination of life throughout the years of my religious life; the sincerity of my own commitment; my search to understand the suffering of Christ; the companionships I have known within religious life and community; the years of delving into the lives of great witnesses of Christian commitment: these were all part of my development, to understand the sacred in life, the revelation of God, the meaning of Christ and the Gospel.

But none of these experiences, events and realities ever questioned my dependencies—challenged the things which I depend on, in life—as did the people with whom I came to 'exist'. Such questioning has remained a permanent aspect of my life to this day. It is strengthened and deepened by the very experience of sharing life with other priests, religious, and lay people who embark on the same questioning. And it is given a daily chance, because my closest religious companions join me and allow me to join them in that questioning.

I 'exist with and suffer with' these people as we grant each other power over our own lives. The suggestion that we should share all we have with those with whom we exist and suffer, for them is but the foolishness of the Gospel— but even the suggestion of such a sharing has within it the seeds of liberation.

That General Chapter Document from 1970 was later revised, and by 1982, we presented it to the governing body of the order as it reads below:

> We read and accept in a spirit of faith and fraternal love the signs of the times, as did St Paul of the Cross who saw the name of Jesus engraved on the foreheads of the poor. Guided by the teachings of the Church, we commit ourselves to justice.

NINETEEN SEVENTY-ONE

We see this as a constitutive element of that evangelisation to which we are called by our dedication to the Passion of Christ who was put to death by our injustices. The hard work involved in such service is an invitation to embrace the cross in a spirit of fidelity to our mission. Our lives should be prophetic protest at the injustices we find. To spread the justice proclaimed on the cross should be the determining criteria in whatever decisions orient our style of life.

2

Searching for a new monasticism

*The failures of asceticism ~ Rationalising our lack
of response to the poor ~ The concern of humanised
religion ~ Asking the wrong questions about being
human ~ Searching for a new ascetic*

The Christian viewpoint of life is rich in its patterns of thought and action, but two fundamental movements are essentially bound up within it. One is the denial of self; the other is a searching and journeying in and through life. In the vision of Christ, this is all summed up in the words 'Deny yourself, lose yourself' and 'come follow me'. If one may paraphrase Christ: 'Discipline your mind, your will and your senses; die to yourself, not for any negative reasons, but that you may take in the values of my interpretation of life.'

This denial is at the heart of the 'ascetic' life. The history of Christianity is the history of that life of denial, and the history of those who accepted the Christ interpretation of life and followed it through to the end. In fact asceticism, as I have described it, is a regular part of human life—when any human being strives for any form of achievement, for example; but if it is to have value and meaning, it must be for the sake of something more.

Passionist life, when I joined it, was institutionally austere—and indeed, the same could be said for many other religious orders, and of the institutional life offered to the person joining the priesthood. When I was young, joining the Passionists was almost looked upon as voluntarily moving to Siberia. It was the way Passionists lived, not the way Passionists acted, which caused the thunderstruck responses. I believe that many religious and priests still live sacrificial and austere lives today, but the austerity does not take its starting point in given institutional frameworks, as it did then.

Yet now I am all too often asked about new structures and new methodologies—what the future of the Church may be*—and the questions are focused upon what can only be described in very generic terms as the loss of that Christian asceticism. Words or phrases like *giving into everything, going soft, loss of penance, do what you like, have it both ways,* are common linguistic coinage for many Christians in my circles.

I believe there is a rightness in these questions; I believe they have a point about the loss of asceticism, and I have sympathy with them in that regard. I, too, feel a helplessness when face-to-face with the question of what the Church should be today. But I find myself having to question the very starting point of the Church's approach to the contemporary world; that the asceticism, or self-emptying we are all called to, will not take the form we know, nor what we expect.

—
* No doubt due to my ten years in the inner city, in what many have called an 'apostolic experiment', although I myself simply call it a mode of religious life and ministry.

We have a long history of Christian asceticism, and although each era picked up what it had inherited, at the same time each era was affected by the moods, tendencies and opinions of its own historical moment. Thus I look into the God revealed in my times and seek to construct a theology in part rooted in the God who is revealed to me *now*; but I also look into my times to search out the reasons, motivations and influences which call me to my self-emptying, to that loss of self.

The asceticism of my early Passionist years was meant to change me—it was meant to be a denial of the self, and it did have a great effect on me. I look back on much of it with gratitude, but I do think that such asceticism actually removed me from seeing and processing the agonies of this world. It has taken many years to reach the position in which I now find myself.

Rationalising our lack of response to the poor

I can only speak for myself, but our institutional asceticism did not awaken in me a passion for the powerless of this world. There was, surely, compassion with the poor; indeed, the sense of compassion in my own order is legendary. But the idea that I must, in some way, participate in their hopelessness; and feel, however vicariously, their pain; and become passionate about the evil done to them by the powerful of this world—this idea did not really impinge on me.

SEARCHING FOR A NEW MONASTICISM

For example, I entered the novitiate of the Passionist congregation only a matter of weeks after that August morning in 1945 when we all awoke to the horror of Hiroshima. Four square miles of a Japanese city had become a raging inferno with a temperature of 6,000°C in a matter of minutes. The atomic bomb had been dropped.

Humanity knew that it had captured and demonstrated a power over its own destiny almost beyond description. If military pundits were to say that war would never be the same again, more humble people would know that peace would never be the same again. Historical generalisations are always dangerous; yet I feel it is true to say that that summer day was the beginning of a new world.

Yet the tragedy of Hiroshima in no way touched my formation. The novitiate house which I joined was a monastery 'nestling', as the vocation literature described it, 'in the foothills of the Cotswolds'. It was a peaceful and sleepy place. I was introduced to an ordered and distinctive routine which had been going on, virtually uninterrupted, for over one hundred and fifty years. The only reminders of the war-torn years were rationing, an intake of ex-servicemen at a fairly intense level, and the presence of German prisoners of war, still in the neighbourhood, not yet repatriated.

Perhaps, like the rest of the world, we all just wanted to forget the Holocaust and the power which humanity had taken to itself. Such well-meaning obliviousness would not last long. Perhaps it was sad that we attempted to turn our face the other way, for humanity in general—and the

Church in particular—were both to be troubled in spirit, and challenged in mind, by this new power over destiny which humanity had taken in its grip. Above all, it would be called to cope with, and live in, a strange twilight of 'contrast experience'—the horrific divide between the deprived and the affluent, the powerless and powerful.

I suppose 'contrast experience' has always been a feature of human existence. Vice and virtue have always been planted and harvested simultaneously. Moonrock can be transported with relative ease to Earth for the curiosity of the scientist, yet grain cannot be moved with a like ease for the feeding of the hungry. We are forced to live with immense wealth and affluence and yet forced to gaze upon degrading poverty and inequality. Even where I now live in the inner city of Liverpool, I have only to drive a few miles to pass from poverty to riches, from powerlessness to power. Has it been worth walking on the moon and neglecting our world? At this level of 'contrast experience', human experiences cannot help but begin to affect theology.

It is always a temptation to rationalise our lack of response to the demands of the poor. You could say in my early days as a priest, the impact of the 'contrast experience' had not fully registered in my life; indeed, it had not been injected into the bloodstream of the world's experience. At the same time, I cannot escape the fact that I used the structures and institutions of religious life to protect me from fully facing up to such sinfulness.

There were exceptions. The priest worker movement made a very great impact upon me, and was a troubling factor in my own conscience. The same could be said when I became more and more involved in the Young Christian Worker movement. But in the latter case, I believe the position of 'being a chaplain' was more important to me than the effort to really understand, and face up to the consequences of, the examples of powerlessness which were presented to me. I was more concerned with helping them to change their vision of life than with allowing them to change my life. They had questions, I had answers.

But questions were beginning to emerge for me. Although we were all very happy Thomists*, the fact that 'feeling' was really part of philosophising made its impact. The cracks were beginning to show, at least on some of the walls of Thomism and what is sometimes called 'Catholic social doctrine'.

Yet even then, I found a subtle escape route from the real question of the powerless; it still had not bitten deep enough to turn into a question of life itself. I escaped into the great concern with 'humanised religion', which sprang from the emergence of theologies of the Incarnation and, above all, the Resurrection.

—
* A philosophical system derived from Thomas Aquinas; Austin implies that his philosophical worldview was neatly ordered, until it was disrupted. [*Ed.*]

The concern of humanised religion

I remember a friend of mine from Holland talking to me one day during the General Chapter of my order in Rome in 1968. It was not an easy Chapter. We were walking in the garden of the mother house on this particular day, and conversation turned to the upheavals in the Dutch Church that had followed the Second World War. He said to me that we did not really understand at all: "You see, you have never seen your fellow countrymen, men, women and children from your own town, put up against a wall and shot after being betrayed by their own countrymen."

After that experience, so many of the Dutch—and indeed the whole continental church—had but one thought in mind. After the era of the concentration camps, only one thing mattered: a new *faith in humanity* had to be discovered. It was not a denial of God; it was a search for God. It was not a rebellion against the Church; it was an effort at purification. Nothing could be allowed to get in the way of re-awakening the goodness, truth and unity buried in the depths of humanity. Dogma was so remote; ecclesiastical authority so far removed from the heartrending urgency and restoration of hopefulness in humanity. After such experiences, Christian consciousness and structure were meaningless unless they were put to the service of restoring again the sacredness of humanity.*

---

* I was reading recently the testimony of Dorota Larska, a Polish communist and a prisoner in Auschwitz. She affirms the sentiments of my Dutch fellow religious. In the course of legal proceedings before a British

This anxiousness to find a new faith in humanity came through very strongly in the Catholic church, almost immediately after the war. It came through both at a magisterial and theological level. In the former case, one has only to recall the never-ending special audiences of Pope Pius XII. Every address appealed for a Christian commitment within the human context. As for the latter, there was a whole development of what came to be called the Theology of the Laity.* The Cardijn† movement, initiated many years before, was given a new boost; a whole new theological terminology came to birth.

Certainly the mood was that no Christian wanted to "pretend we are human", as Osborne's Jimmy Porter said, in *Look Back in Anger*. Rather, we all wanted to fulfil Jimmy's longing:

> Oh heavens, how I long for a little ordinary human enthusiasm. Just enthusiasm that's all. I want to hear a warm, thrilling voice cry out Hallelujah! Hallelujah! I'm alive.

And if we found ourselves put off by such exhortations to the charismatic, we at least wanted to make it clear to

—

court, she was asked whether she would have taken part in experimental operations, if she had been ordered to do so. In her reply, she referred to the comments of a fellow prisoner, Dr Hautval: that no one who had witnessed the medical experiments performed in the camp would be allowed to survive, and that 'the only thing that is left for us is to behave, for the rest of the short time left to us, like human beings.'

* Giving greater significance to the role and experiences of the non-ordained majority in the church.

† The Young Trade Unionists, which became the worldwide Young Christian Workers.

PASSION FOR THE INNER CITY

the same Jimmy that he had a totally false dilemma in mind when he said to Helena:

> And if you can't bear the thought of messing up your nice clean soul, you'd better give up the whole idea of life and become a saint. Because you'll never make it as a human being. It's either this world or the next.

This orientation of theological thinking, and consequent pastoral method, has not lost momentum. I would go so far as to say that after Vatican II the momentum was increased. The calling of the Second Vatican Council, and the theologians of the day, made it an exciting time to be a young priest. For my part, I was discovering the potential glory of the human; but I failed, as yet, to see the wounds of the human.*

And as the cry of the poor became louder, like many others I began to realise that this human reality had much more to say to us. Always conscious of the priest worker movement, conscious too of the social reality which the Church had presented to the world for many years in official teaching, I believe it was only really a matter of facing up to what had niggled away for so long. Once one's mind was turned to one's own world, and its urban chaos, we realised that much more was being demanded of us all than had appeared at first sight.

---

* In fact I think these theologies helped more to 'humanise theology' than to 'theologise humanity': there was a tendency to 'consecrate every human thing in sight'.

SEARCHING FOR A NEW MONASTICISM

As the Vatican Council piloted itself through the rather rough seas of a new world, the debate in religious circles concerning the meaning of 'lifestyle' got under way*. As Fr Congar wrote:

> In a church which has really become again the church of the poor, the rich will find and take their place; but the poor will never find and take their place in the church of the rich...
>
> *The practical rediscovery of evangelical poverty* is linked to the absolute value of love, of agape, beyond all moralism, and to the value of service, responsibility and witness. It owes much to the determination not to live for oneself alone, but to be with others, particularly with the poorest, to put oneself 'at the centre of distress, in the heart of misery', to enter into a communal relationship with the deprived. It is decisively bound up with the rediscovery of the values of Christian existence or ontology, beyond the moralism or legalism so frequently denounced at the Council. [1]

The Church was facing an ascetical question, going to the heart of the institutional and structural elements of priesthood and religious life—the same question posed by the priest worker witness of the forties and fifties. The question was: *how can our structures be changed to facilitate the release of the passion for the poor?*

Though ultimately any change is dependent on the will of the community and the individual, in all gentleness I would

---

* Which is to say, how these changes in theological thinking should be lived out in practical terms.

think this question can still be asked of the ministerial church and religious life. For me, it is the most profound question for a Church of credibility in the future. The pain of the 'contrast experience' of our times is calling us to a purgation which is critical for the development of the Christian community.

Asking the wrong questions about being human

Perhaps all this may be called just my opinion, and that is fair enough. But if new ideas and endeavours are to say something to more traditional ways, then those involved in the new have an obligation, in Christian love and friendship, to speak and act with all honesty and without hysterics or insensitivity—and conscious of the classic problem of splinters in the eye*, which I hope I am.

I believe the Church has asked the wrong question about being human. It has chosen the wrong starting point. All too often, we have seen the entrance into 'the human' as a technique, or a methodology. We have been led to where the action is, and not to where the life is. A true discovery of 'the human' could lead us along a joyous path to the crucified God, with a realism at once ecstatically joyful and excruciatingly painful; a new, very profound and positive

---

* Matthew 7:1-5

asceticism. It could lead us to rediscover the radical and challenging meaning of 'the Crucified'.

I believe it to be true that if you have not suffered because of Christianity, then you have never known Christianity. The radical question is *how* to suffer. The question of 'existence with', is not mere physical existence with; authentic 'existence with' is about reflection, and contemplation, and above all about exploring, with humanity, the problems and the potential of the human heart. It is from this exploration that all else will emerge. Prayer will not be seen merely as the 'given necessity' of Christian existence, but will emerge from the depth of a shared life experience. It is in understanding and living out the meaning of 'existence with and suffering with' that one is brought to authentic Christian dependency.

Bertrand Russell writes:

> Three Passions, simple but overwhelmingly strong have governed my life: the longing for love, the search for knowledge, and unbearable pity for the suffering of mankind. These passions, like great winds, have blown me hither and thither, in a wayward course, over a deep ocean of anguish, reaching to the very verge of despair... Love and knowledge, so far as they were possible, led upwards towards the heavens. But always pity brought me back to earth. Echoes of cries of pain reverberate in my heart. Children in famine, victims tortured by oppressors, helpless old people a burden to their sons, and the whole world of loneliness, poverty and pain make a mockery of what human life should be. I long to alleviate the evil, but I cannot, and I too suffer.[2]

PASSION FOR THE INNER CITY

Any human being reaching for nobility of life, any saint claiming to take the gospel seriously and any mystic wishing to witness to the unique union with God, could take these words of Russell without fear, and make them his own. I may interpret the nature, the quality and the intensity of the love and knowledge differently; but my formation as a Catholic child, and later as a young man in the religious life and priesthood, was indeed governed by a longing for love and a search for knowledge.

Based upon an understanding and a love of an incarnate God, the search had to plunge me back into the highways of human strengths and weaknesses; but as I have said, I think I was somewhat protected, even in those latter years, from hearing the 'echoes of cries of pain' of the poor of this world. I do not think 'the whole world of loneliness, poverty and pain' sufficiently impinged upon my intellect and will.

Christian apologists may say that though loneliness, poverty and pain are to be regretted and condemned, they nevertheless have brought the best out in humanity, and unlike Russell they may say that the whole point of the Christian faith, face-to-face with such a tattered world, is to make sure I do not dawdle at the verge of despair. For two major reasons I resist such qualifications. First, I would stress the fact that one cannot come to grips with the meaning of real Christian hope, without simultaneously coming face-to-face with the stark reality of human suffering.

Secondly, too many qualifications have the habit of pushing aside the major thought. The idea of 'sinfulness'— which is basically a state of selfishness—becomes far too abstract a matter, rather than something which is demonstrated by the loneliness, the poverty and the pain of human beings. We search for a knowledge of the creator, but not of creation. I think this happens far too often in Christian reflections upon human affairs. At this stage of my religious life, when I attempt to search for knowledge and long for love, I cannot escape the unbearable pity with the lonely, the poor and suffering of this world. It totally governs, determines and purgates that search and longing.

This is not something merely emotional. It is a dimension of human existence too long neglected in philosophical and theological matters. Although, if the poverty situation of our world does *not* break down the doors of humanity at an emotional level, it has very little chance of capturing the human person at an intellectual and volitional level. My pity has led me to ask hard questions both on the dimension of consciousness and structure of Faith and the Church, not to mention the spiritual and moral bankruptcy of our social, political and economic consciousness. Far from driving me into a prison of absurd obsessions and personal prejudices, such questioning—and the engagement with life which the questioning has led to—has liberated me into a fresh life of faith, religious commitment and priesthood. The question of poverty has turned out to be for me much larger than poverty. Rahner writes:

> The history of religious life throughout the two millennia of its existence has been, one might almost be justified in saying, a constant record of shifts in the interpretation of poverty in itself... Historically speaking, therefore, we have to recognise fully the existence of these very different motivations in the numerous movements towards poverty; and controversies

> about poverty (all reform movements in the religious orders and all controversies have in fact always entailed disputes about poverty too, and these go far beyond the dispute in the Franciscan order). History, therefore, fully justifies us in refusing to strive for an absolutely univocal explanation when we come to investigate the theological meaning and motivation of poverty. It is to be expected *a priori* that the poverty practised in all religious orders is a relatively complex phenomenon, which, as practised in the concrete, is quite incapable of being reduced to any one theological root.[3]

I would be the last to deny the complexity which Rahner so rightly presents. Religious life and priesthood have agonised about the meaning of poverty, but the debate has too often distracted us from certain basic facts or experiences. The facts and experiences being that there are millions who are powerless over destiny because the ideologies and structures of our world, created and propagated by the powerful, effectively deny them the chances of developing their God-given greatness as persons. Has the debate been an escape route for me? I must admit that it has. I do not think that my passion for the poor has been so fundamental to my life that it has conditioned all my knowing and loving.

Searching for a new ascetic

Contemporary theology and church teaching have stressed the need to discover God anew in the era in which I live. My 'following' must, in the right sense, be truly contemporary. To be sure, Russell's 'passions'—the search

SEARCHING FOR A NEW MONASTICISM

for knowledge, and the longing to love and be loved by creator and creation—are fundamental to Christian life. But I must ask myself, in this era and in this inner city, what are to be my grounds for asceticism? What will my self-emptying be in aid of? Is there another passion now in my life crying out to be satisfied?

I believe that passion to be in the pity for the loneliness, the poverty, and the pain of the powerless in the inner city. I have personalised this question, but I believe this is the road into which the church is called to journey. Thus the poverty question is not just one aspect of apostolic life, but absolutely essential for an interpretation of human life in the light of the revelation of Jesus.

I believe that I face a vast self-emptying of all kinds of values and structures which I once believed were essential to religious life and priesthood. I believe the 'contrast experience' in which we live is calling us to a new, radicalised Christian life; and without facing up to this question of powerlessness, we shall not find out how to 'follow anew' and therefore develop God's creation.

This is what the inner city has done to me; and like all Christian life, it has been an experience of pain and joy. I feel I have been led to search out and understand a new ascetic and I find myself, with all gentleness, having to ask my fellow Christians whether we are asking the right questions. Mindful of the qualifications which must be understood, I can do no better than quote the words of Pere Loew:

PASSION FOR THE INNER CITY

I have retraced the story of the missionary effort pursued at Marseilles and noted its principal stages in order that, drawing from the facts themselves, I might one by one mark off the definite conclusions reached.

What emerges? First the necessity for regarding man not under this or that aspect, but in the totality of his life, good and bad alike. In this way one keeps well clear of sterile discussions on the different activities of this apostolate or their order of importance.

Then comes the need for adopting a way of life which will bring back the healthy members of the Community, and particularly Christians, both clergy and faithful, into the main stream of human life... Next, the need for sharing the troubles and anxieties of work, and injustices of the labour-contract system, living with the workers and their families...

But at the same time it is clear we must provide action at the required level, seeking to understand,... so as to apply the remedy ... to the very root of the disorder...

If, then, we want to define concisely what services must be assumed by the missionary apostolate as a whole, how much is to be given to the claims of friendship, how much to preaching the Gospel, how much to spontaneity and how much to organisation, if we want... 'neither to fish with a line, nor fish with a net, but to change the water in the pond', we must begin by analysing as accurately as possible the essential features characterising the great urban centres and their repercussions on the lives of the men and families living there. [4]

3

Losing our assumptions

*Rethinking where prayer comes from ~ What past ruins
can teach us about a failure of reflection*

I was eleven years of age when the Second World War
began. In spite of my age I remember those years very
distinctly. But there is one memory above all. The war had
not been going on for long when the 'Prayers for Peace'
were made a structural part of our church services. And I
remember going home to my father to ask him if there were
Catholics in Germany, and being assured that the Catholic
Church did not stop at the English Channel—indeed, that
it got better the further you travelled into Europe. I asked
my puzzled father whether the Germans were keen to win
the war, and he vaguely thought they were. Inevitably my
questions went on. Would the Germans be praying for
peace? Did they see peace as them winning the war and
beating us? And so on.

I am well aware now that this kind of questioning has
been woven into wise sayings about whose side God is
on. But that is later knowledge for me. At that time in
my life it troubled me, not only about prayer, but about
God's puzzlement. Later on, I remember priests going to

prisoner-of-war camps 'to say Mass', and that increased my puzzlement. Somehow or other it seemed that prayer became a kind of government-and-opposition within the divine economy: who could push God one way or the other? Who could operate the spiritual filibuster more adroitly?

Naive? To be sure it is. Sophistication has taken over since. But the divine parliamentary battle seems still to go on. This approach to prayer can still worm its spiritual way into the soul. Indeed I think there is much that encourages it along.

The exhortation to pray is well founded in the Christian tradition. And one thing is certain: if you are a Christian, you can hardly be against prayer. But the real problem, it seems to me is how you are really going to be *for* prayer. In saying this I am not broaching the nature of private, public, group, charismatic, liturgical, or meditative prayer— in other words, I am not concerned with the way 'prayer comes out'. The question is more: what does prayer arise from, whence does it come?

From the moment I stepped across the threshold of the novitiate, everyone with the right and the expertise to remind me of the nature of my Christian life has called me to prayer. Indeed, 'call' might be too soft a word. Retreat-masters, bishops, priests, and religious have all, at some time or other, warned me of the dire consequences of a life without prayer. Indeed, since I have occupied a Retreat Master's chair and a pulpit for a good chunk of life, I have been part of the persuasion.

LOSING OUR ASSUMPTIONS

In my novitiate and student days, and indeed in the later years, over seven hours a day were given over to various duties in the church, praying. In the novitiate, I went through all kinds of exercises to teach me to pray. Meditation for two hours a day was a focal point of my life. And I would be called to give an account, publicly, of my meditation. I actually saw people sleep through a whole hour, and I slept myself, and then rose to paint a graphic picture of the time I had spent with Christ during the hours of his agony. I rebuilt Jerusalem with an alacrity which would put to shame any contemporary tourist guide.

When things were going wrong in the religious life, inevitably someone would come along, even from as far away as Rome, and pass out warnings about the dreadful state of prayer. All too often I was told that there was not enough prayer going on in the community: if it did not quicken in tempo and pace then the whole thing would fall apart. The consequences would be beyond the most fertile imagination.

Now—only God looks into the human soul. But all too often, having listened to such dire warnings, and accepting the fact that my view of my brethren could be very superficial, it did strike me that they remained good, struggling men. They certainly did not seem to be getting in the way of God's plan and they did not, for sure, go hurtling down a terrible slope of moral decline. They seemed happy and content; they went about their lives in gentle service. I have been told more than once even in recent days—and I wrestle with the accusation—that the reason for a total fall in vocations* is to be found in a lack of prayer. Actually, I cannot do much more praying than I do, so I resent such a criticism. I would be inclined to ask whether we are praying for the development of the *right kind* of priesthood and religious life; but that is for future reflection.

Suffice it to say at this moment that every single call to reform or renewal demands prayer as an absolute necessity. I simply cast doubt on such a starting point, or better I ask: from what shall prayer come? From the midst of the desert? From the horror of the city? Deserts and cities are just contexts of life. The pure heart? He who seeks the will of God? The will and the heart need something to uphold and inform them.

In prayer, we seek to ask God for the wisdom which will lead us deeper into his creative and redemptive plan. I look at my stumbling, and the model of Jesus' life, and in prayer I attempt to articulate my failure to deepen my reflection. This, I think, is what the whole Christian community is about in its moment of liturgical celebration. It is about finding, and expressing, and seeking help to develop, those values which Jesus listed as necessary for the development of peace, holiness, justice and truth. But crucially, it is also about deepening *reflection* and the integration of values into life. Without that prelude of reflection, the entire performance of life is aborted.

---

* That is, the number of people being initiated into monastic life in England and Wales.

LOSING OUR ASSUMPTIONS

What past ruins can teach us about a failure of reflection

My room is a jumble of many things. I sit in the midst of it now, in the inner city. Books predominate, but two in particular are important possessions.

One is fairly valuable. It is Dugdale's *Monasticon Anglicanum*, which is a primary source for the religious houses of pre-Reformation Britain. The other possession is without any intrinsic value. It is simply a cheap and little gallery of L.S. Lowry prints. I am, by profession, neither monastic historian nor art connoisseur; though I would have more expertise in the former than in the latter. Leaving aside all expertise in the areas of art and monastic history, they both say something to me each day which is substantially the same. They are daily reminders of the 'tale of two ruins'. Let us have a look first of all at the *Monasticon Anglicanum*.

In 1132, the Prior of St Mary's Abbey, in York, along with eleven other monks, departed from the Abbey in order to begin another one: Fountains Abbey. They departed after much debate and acrimony. The central issue, not for the first or last time in religious life history, was the spiritual energy crisis at St Mary's. Prior Richard, the spokesman of the protest, more or less summed up the problem.

> We intend no rebellion, Father Abbot. It is simply a matter of our desire to fulfil the rule of our Father Benedict, and even

PASSION FOR THE INNER CITY

more important, to live fully the ancient rule of the gospel of Jesus Christ... We wish to follow the poor Christ in our voluntary poverty, to carry the crucified Christ in our bodies; we will not be impeded from seeking true evangelical peace.

Yet the Abbey Richard and his companions went out to develop, and did develop, went the same way as St Mary's York, four hundred years after their departure. In 1537, William Thirsk, then Abbot of Fountains Abbey, was executed for taking part in the Pilgrimage of Grace.* Two years later, on 26 November 1539, Fountains Abbey was surrendered to the King's men† by the new Abbot and thirty-one priests.

These were years of a very distinct crisis in Christendom, one much bigger than the attack upon monastic life: they were the climactic years of the Reformation, between 1534 and 1540. There was persecution at work, both physical and mental.

From 1066 to the year 1540, the number of religious houses in England and Wales had grown from 61 to nearly 850, with a population of around 10,000 religious. Then in 1540, roughly 8,500 religious were put out of their houses. Accepting all the horrific aspects of those years, conscious

---

* A popular uprising in Yorkshire and Northern England in 1536: a mass protest of Henry VIII's dissolution of the monasteries, against a background of cruel taxation and forced enclosures by the aristocratic class which had exiled people from the land on which they subsisted.

† The King in question being Henry VIII again, whose orders were enacted by the agents of Thomas Cromwell. The monastery and its land were then 'sold' to a rich merchant, in the sense that the King was paid for the property over which he had forcibly claimed ownership.

of our own weakness, and thus being very careful about harsh judgement, it nevertheless remains quite stunning that over five hundred years of religious life and history could be dismantled in a matter of five or six years. To be sure, there was the confusion of the times. Communication was not what we expect now. The persecution, too, was violent. But the question should be asked: how many of those religious in any way saw the signs of the time?

It is agreed that they were not all evil people; like the rest of us, they were average athletes in God's service. Vast immorality in the religious houses is now seen as spurious history.*

Certain reformers, both past and present, have taken them to task about their life of prayer. I would suggest, however, that failure rested more in reflection than in prayer. Indeed, many of the debates which had marked the history of religious life were far removed from the daily comings and goings of a world in process of change.

I would suggest that this tale of ruin had its roots not in immorality, but in a failure of awareness. Things just went on, and it was assumed things would carry on going. There is a charming story, touched with terrible sadness in

---

* Austin perhaps overestimates the average person's familiarity with this era and its analysis. But it's probably widely understood that the monarchy's own motives were far from pure. Monasteries had become rich landowners by this point; by seizing and selling their land, the Crown gained a huge income and funded its military campaigns. Certainly the wealth of the monasteries might be seen as a betrayal of principle in itself, but it seems likely, as Austin implies, that most monks had become complacent, rather than particularly seditious or wildly immoral. [Ed.]

view of the times which were to come, told by Knowles. It is contained in a letter of one monk to another written, as Knowles says, 'On a spring morning when April was tossing bounty to the cherries in the Vale of Evesham'.

> See the air is mild, and the breeze light from the west; the thickets ring with bird song, and are merry with the sight and scent of blossom. Up, then! Drop Scotus, take up your bowls and be off to the green: you will bring back a bushel of health as well as a sixpence or two. If you don't feel like bowls, go fishing.[1]

Indeed, it may have been a spring morning. It was also the eve of a tragic spiritual winter.

The failure of dynamism of religious life had long been underway before Henry VIII's marriage became a factor. The failure was a disease of Christendom. It was not peculiarly British. The debates of Bernard of Clairvaux and Cluny, centred upon riches and arches and poor furnishings, were dreadfully insignificant in a world which was reaching an era of evolutionary change in urban living and scholastic learning.

Abbeys like Fountains, with wide-eyed vision for a new future, abbeys which looked to witness to the poverty of Jesus, soon found in their very success the seeds of their failure. The curse of development was wedded to security. Security in its turn bred an obsession with all that was within, with themselves. Not many years passed before such regulations as the following found their way into a statute book;

LOSING OUR ASSUMPTIONS

Pig-styes can be two or even three leagues from the grange, but pigs, though they can wander by day, must return to the styes at night. Swineherds and shepherds must get their daily food from their abbey or grange.[2]

We of another era should not laugh too quickly, or if we laugh let us laugh at ourselves. Early Christian foolishness inevitably gets caught in a later sweet and worldly reasonableness. Its roots of failure must be found not so much in its own care for structure. It is more a question of one's vision of life being blinkered by self-preservation.

God knows only too well that in his name anything can be justified. The greatest vision can be reduced to the backyard view of the one who will not look beyond his own self-preservation. Francis of Assisi, who pitched for the absolute to become one of the poorest of his fellowmen, suffered the same fate at the hands of disciples and commentators. If it is possible, a shiver must have gone up his sanctified spine as he listened in Heaven to a sermon preached at Pisa in 1261. He had hardly settled down to enjoying his status of canonisation when he could hear on earth the Archbishop of Pisa preaching this incredible message:

How pleasing it must be for merchants to know that one of their cohorts, St. Francis, was a merchant and was also made a saint in our time. Oh how much good hope there must be for merchants who have such a merchant intermediary with God.[3]

This would be excusable. For many a preacher knows too well the problem of trying to find the right thing to say to

PASSION FOR THE INNER CITY

the wrong audience about the right saint. The trouble was that even amongst Francis' disciples such a matter would soon be open to debate. In fact those who longed for a radical poverty, believing this was the life of Francis and his message, found themselves in the unbelievable predicament of being burnt to death as heretics.

But whence came the ruins? I believe they came from a total absence of reflection. It is this reflection which must be deeper than prayer. I accept that one can reflect without praying; but if there is to be authentic prayer life, there must be reflection.

4

Rediscovering reflection

*Lessons from modern ruins ~ A contemplative life
without 'going away' ~ 'Existence with' and reflection are
mutually necessary*

I should make it clear at this point that I in no way wish to
suggest that all reflection must be of a profound academic
nature. The profundity of speculation and education may
make a difference to one's reflection, but there can be
reflection without such qualities.*

There is a danger of equating the experience and exercise
of reflection with intellectual capability—intellectual
capability, that is, of the kind associated with the academic
mind. This is not the reflection I mean. I have known great
academics without the slightest depth in their reflection
upon life; and I have known, both in my life in the inner city
and in my prison-work experience, people who are illiterate
but whose depth of reflection is quite astonishing. Too
often, in our Christian world, the 'middle-management'
theology of the pulpit has failed to encourage—even
effectively suppressed—this capacity for reflection of the
'ordinary' person.

—

* If you read the English mystic Julian of Norwich, for example, you are very
conscious of an unlettered person, but not of a person without reflection.

I stated that the ruins of the past came from an absence of reflection. If I personally come to this conclusion through my own present religious life and priestly experience—and through my amateur journeying into the past—my life here in the inner city, in the midst of another ruin, drives me to the identical conclusion.

I have mentioned the *Monasticon Anglicanum*; I look now to my book of Lowry prints. I see factory smoke hanging upon the industrial air. I look to a snow-covered industrial scene. Little figures pass the factory gate; the crowd move about the cornershop. In the inner city I feel I am always in Lowry country; I drive to my job at the local prison every day along a derelict dock road.

It was all born of an era which spoke of wealth, prosperity and progress. In fact, another harvest was soon reaped. Terraced houses turned into slums, in spite of the heroic struggle of a people. Dock cranes hanging idle over abandoned dockyards; a people prematurely aged; city youngsters emerging from school without hope for tomorrow; pathetic panic to save the inner city; mills boarded up, and grass growing in the gutters.

It is all too close to us to treat them as we would the ruin of the Abbey. They do not invite the picnic party. Sunset can be beautiful over such ruins, but the ruins distract from the hope which is to be found in the sunset, for they deny that things will be better at sunrise. As I go into residents' groups and as I participate in community meetings of the neighbourhood, I find myself with the same question, 'Did enough people attempt to think into a future? Did they look at the movement of a world around them? Was there any depth of reflection?'

Once, the slave ships moved in and out of Liverpool. The names of the local streets ironically tell the tale of slavery. Did anyone then think about the harvest of bitterness and racism we were sowing? It is not yet the time to consider in depth, but I must ask the question now. How many in the powerful (and powerful it was in numbers) Catholic Church in Liverpool, reflected in order to prepare for another era?

There was prayer in the Abbey, there was prayer in the city. But whence came that prayer? I say all this for a crucial reason. When I speak of 'existence with', it is meaningless without reflection. The 'existence with' which I have in mind causes contemplation, and contemplation deepens the meaning of 'existence with'. In fact 'existence with', as I understand it in these pages, is by its very nature a contemplative life.

A contemplative life without 'going away'

I am told that having no answers—only questions—is essential for contemporary wisdom. I would think that largely depends on one's background. If you have been fed with banquets of certitude, suffered from indigestion, or even worse from hunger, you cannot help wondering about your diet.

In the summer of 1980, I was asked to give some talks in America to contemplative sisters. I had come from a series of lectures on 'The Church, Religious Life and Social

PASSION FOR THE INNER CITY

Suffering'. Part of these lectures were given to sisters who were severely handicapped. I found it an enriching time; my lectures were based upon my experience in the inner city, but everything strangely and wonderfully came together in a common understanding of powerlessness. Their appeal was not for a cure by prayer or healing; it was rather to deepen their understanding of suffering.

The location I came to after these lectures was beautiful beyond belief; the environmental peace and quiet was balm to my own soul. However, it was not long before I became troubled in spirit and I began to long for home. It was not the longing rooted in the commonly experienced state of homesickness. I felt so completely lost and unreal without the daily hopefulness painfully kept alive in the midst of the inner city. I tried to turn my mind to other things, putting off emerging questions about this 'contemplative life' taking place in this wonderful and glorious setting of creation.

Let me come clean: had any Christian the right to such a mode of discovering God? This is the question which kept on troubling me. It was at this stage that one night I rediscovered Thomas Merton.* It was a letter written,

---

* I had never been a particularly devoted Thomas Merton fan, but he certainly influenced my life at this stage. He was the first 'modern' to demonstrate publicly with great articulation and power, a return to the ancient. It was a shock to hear about one who had known the era of the big band and jazz and all that, deciding upon that mysterious life called the Trappist. We had all seen people 'going away' (how we betray ourselves in language), to be nuns and priests and brothers. We had even heard about a few going away to be monks, but there was something extreme about Merton. The world and the cloister were starkly set in opposition by his

52

REDISCOVERING REFLECTION

in haste he assures us, in the August of 1967. The letter is addressed to the Abbot of the Cistercian monastery of Frattocchie near Rome, and the purpose of the letter is to respond to a request made by Paul VI, who had asked for a message from contemplatives to the world. Merton is reluctant even to attempt such a letter, and writes:

> The problem of the contemplative orders is a problem of great ambiguity. People look at us, recognise we are sincere, recognise that we have indeed found a certain peace, and see after all that there may be some worth to it: but can we convince them that this means anything to them? I mean, can we convince them professionally and collectively, as 'the contemplatives' in our walled institution, that what our institutional life represents has any meaning for them? If I were absolutely confident in answering yes to this, then it would be simple to draft the message we are asked to draw up. But to me, at least, it is not that simple, and for that reason I am perhaps disqualified from participating in this at all. In fact, this preface is in part a plea to be left out, to be exempted from a task to which I do not in the least recognise myself equal.[1]

I would also, and did in that situation, find it difficult to address my brothers and sisters in the world. In that situation, like Merton, I felt myself, as he says,

---

early writing. He was so classical an example of rejection and commitment. First there was the conversion to Roman Catholicism only to be followed by another conversion into that silent unknown which the name Cistercian summoned up.

immensely privileged to be exempt from so many, so very many, of his (the brother in the world's) responsibilities and sufferings.

Yet I have always, since the Poor Clare convent and the Carmelite monastery were pointed out to me as a child, assumed that this way of life is an authentic Christian way; and my purpose is not to enter into any kind of polemic with regard to the rightness or wrongness of such a mode of existence. It is my purpose to come to the point that 'going into' must lead to a profound contemplative life equal to that which is described as 'going away'. Merton helps me further when he says:

> Can I tell you that I have found the answers to the questions that torment the man of our time? I do not know if I have found the answers. When I first became a monk, yes, I was sure of answers. But as I grow old in the monastic life and advance further into solitude, I become aware that I have only begun to seek the questions. And what are the questions? Can man make sense out of his existence? Can man honestly give his life meaning merely by adopting a certain set of explanations which pretend to tell him where the world began and where it will end, why there is evil and what is necessary for a good life? My brother, perhaps in my solitude I have become as it were an explorer for you, a searcher in realms which you are not able to visit—except perhaps in the company of your psychiatrist. I have been summoned to explore a desert area of man's heart in which explanations no longer suffice, and in which one learns that only experience counts.[2]

Merton helped me at that moment on two levels. Contemplation is a quest, not a discovery; it is 'going after' something, not gaping at something, or someone. But deeper still, a Christian contemplative is called to find union with God through journeying also into what Merton calls

> a desert of man's heart, an arid, rocky, dark land of the soul, sometimes illuminated by strange fires which men fear and peopled by spectres men studiously avoid except in their nightmares. And in this area I have learned that one cannot truly know hope unless he has found out how like despair hope is. The language of Christianity has said this for centuries in other less naked terms. But the language of Christianity has been so used and so misused that sometimes you distrust it; you do not know whether or not behind the word cross there stands the experience of mercy and salvation, or only the threat of punishment. If my words mean anything to you I can say to you that I have experienced the cross to mean mercy and not cruelty, truth not deception; that the news of the truth and love of Jesus is indeed good news, but in our time it speaks out in strange places. And perhaps it speaks out in you more than in me; perhaps Christ is nearer to you than he is to me.[3]

In a word, my brother and sister are essential to contemplation, and the 'experience of experiencing' must be taken seriously in Christian life, especially when this implies experiencing in some way the existence and the suffering of the other. Indeed the truth of Jesus speaks out in strange places. Even in the daily dereliction of my inner city and in the joyful hope of the people whom I am privileged to 'exist with' and with whom I attempt to suffer. For in it all there is a sacredness which leads you by the hand to God, and each day I rise to new questions; yesterday's answers simply will not do.

I would be part of Merton's hesitant approach. Can I tell you, my brothers and sisters in the religious life, that I have found answers? Ten years ago I believed I had answers to the Church's mission in the inner city; now I have more questions. The answer, in some sense, rests in the need for a journey to be made, a journey into the centre of our hearts together. My problem and my hope and excitement is in the fact that I must make that journey into the human heart with my brothers and sisters in the inner city. How am I to face up to that journey?

Loneliness there is bound to be in life, solitude there must be. It is not the solitude of a luxury island, but that solitude lived out in the midst of human life, which asks one to face oneself. You see, in the inner city of Liverpool I have found a greater closeness to the Jesus reality, both in crucifixion and hope, than I have ever in the acceptable lands of Christian ministry.

What has brought me to this? This is where I struggle to make my link. It is very simply the reality and experience of 'existence with'. Let me for a moment return to Maritain.

> To exist with, is an ethical category. It does not mean to live with someone in a physical sense, or in the same way he does; it does not mean loving someone in the mere sense of wishing him well; it means loving someone in the sense of becoming

one with him, of bearing his burdens, of living a common moral life with him, of feeling with him and suffering with him.[4]

'Existence with' and reflection are mutually necessary

To Maritain I would have to say: Yes, and No. It has been crucial for me to be in the actual physical conditions of an inner city situation to understand what I can only call the urban task, and it has been crucial for me to do that without the acceptable appendages of ecclesiastical structures. I believe this aspect of what has been called an 'experiment' must be given priority if ministerial renewal is to come about in the Church. At the same time, the 'existence with' must do more than simply put one in the position of physical proximity. There is no point whatsoever in building a theory for religious life and priesthood on the simple act of physical existence in an area of social malaise. As Loew says:

> This is where the real social and religious problems are to be met—not in complicated theoretical abstractions, but in the simple questions devolving on lice and such things.[5]

Loew is not simply dismissing 'theoretical abstractions' in themselves; then he would simply be describing the subtle luxury of being rich enough to live like the poor. Loew is saying that the reflective Christian ministerial existence

PASSION FOR THE INNER CITY

must begin at the point of the lice; authentic 'existence with' must also be bound up with reflection.

Equally, I would argue there is no possibility of authentic reflection without the experience of 'existence with', for it is this which must push back the religious or the priest into the depths of his own soul. This experience of being pushed back is because he or she has agreed to embark on life's journey with 'the other'. The mutual heart searching is not merely to withdraw into the self and to remain there in depressed isolation; it is rather that there may be a journey back into the building of a new world, in the values of Jesus. I believe that this is, in essence, a contemplative existence.

Contemplative life is about knowledge, about union and about love; wrapped up in it is prayer, reflection and dialogue! At the heart of it there must be joy and sorrow, suffering and contentment, ease and pain and the ultimate object of it all is union with God.

My personal attempt to 'exist with' and therefore my 'suffering with' has led me into a contemplative life, and into a solitude which on the one hand shows me God more clearly, yet on the other hand calls for a spiritual stripping in priesthood and religious life which I see essential for the development of a renewed ministerial Church. Above all things I have been forced to ask a very simple yet fundamental question: What are my dependencies in life? As a priest and religious, upon what am I dependent? What is it that prospers and sustains the priesthood and the religious life of today? Or, to put it more broadly, if we seek a Church that is authentically human with the humanity of Jesus, what must we accept as fundamental to such a Church?

Within the Catholic church, there has certainly been institutional reform, following the Second Vatican Council of 1962. But the reform has remained vague. We have undertaken consultations; sought to be more democratic; we have attempted to understand new modes of caring for people, such as community development. Above all, we have assumed that changing modes of action will usher in a new era. At my stage of life I sympathise with all this readily enough. I understand it. I came to the inner city with these ideas uppermost in my mind. Yet, almost against my will, I have been led on to other paths. They may not be the right paths—and they are paths which I might call frightening, albeit with a 'fear' more like the wonderful 'fear of God'. I have been led to the need for a purgation for which there was no ready-made, familiar Christian formula. Action there must be, of course; but, for me, the point is to be initiated in the order of existence, not in the order of action.

As should be very obvious by now, I am not writing a treatise on prayer. My reason for introducing the question of prayer here is simple. The prayer exercise and experience is too easily and superficially invoked as the *sine qua non* of any personal or communal radicalisation of life. The question: *From what shall prayer emerge?*, can all too easily be neglected. Moreover, prayer is an expression of dependency—the articulation of a creature's dependency on his creator.

No Christian will quarrel with this. But, faced with the need for radical reform, I would prefer to speak in terms of 'revolution' within the Church. For a Christian to concentrate upon this one area of dependency, prayer, would be irresponsible—and yet, all too often, this is what happens. Indeed, for many it remains the central issue. 'If only we got down to our prayers, all would be well': reflections like that, uttered with deep sincerity, in the long run help neither God nor man.

I have used the word *reflection* as the basic principle for a beginning and on-going development of Christian vitality. And I have, I hope, made it clear that only with reflection can there be an authentic 'existence with' the world. 'Existence with'—the very basis of what I think and believe—is a very profound fact and experience, from which everything must emerge. Furthermore, when this is understood, one comes to deeper dependencies without which there can be no radicalisation—indeed, no real prayer or articulation of one's dependency upon God.

5

Losing the institutional mind

*Life is complicated ~ How Christian structures lose their
vitality ~ How structures and institutions create the
'institutional mind'*

In the autumn of 1968, before the inner city Mission
began, I arrived in Rome as a delegate to the extraordinary
General Chapter of my order. The chapter was called
extraordinary because it was specifically called to make
decisions about the future life of the order in the light of
the Second Vatican Council. One of its jobs would be to
write a new charter or rule for the Order.

Could one expect anything but a season of storms? If one
was realistic, the answer was yes, and a season of storms we
sailed into. This Chapter, broken into two sessions, lasted
nearly six months. If one takes into account the periods of
time between the first and second session, the span of time
was two years, 1968-1970. I would say the second session
was more difficult than the first. This could be expected,
for pain in human groups always increases the nearer one
comes to the necessity for concrete decision.

During that second session, I was President of the
Commission for Apostolic Reform. In such a situation, it
came home more and more to me how impossible it is to
find formulae, except of the most general kind, which will

61

be relevant to the situation of different regions, nations and cultures, not to mention the variations which necessarily exist in such social and geographical categories. It could be said that the fact that any formulae were found was an effort of genius. It may be equally held, however, that such a success was rather a deep sign of weakness. Arguments went on through the night and into the early morning, and I certainly came to my own conclusion about the 'Voting Board'. I must explain that.

When we first arrived in Rome and made our way to the main hall, we were met by a sign of technological enthusiasm. There were wires all over the place leading into a little box which, when a lever was pulled, set off a board. On this board were five words: *SI, NON, JUXTA MODUM, ABST**. Thus I could use the lever at my little desk to vote on a proposition, and it eventually registered on the board. The board itself caused a controversy. After all, Chapter voting had been run successfully for a good number of years, and this gadget was an insecurity-provoking sign of the times. Thus it took a rather long time to get a large number of intelligent men to learn to press the right button.

A layman was guiding us through this. He eventually handed it over to the President of the Chapter, who invoked a certain measure of spiritual strong-arm pressure to get everyone to catch on with a bit more speed. But the longer the Chapter went on, the more affectionate I became toward that space connected to my little switch called *juxta modum*.

—

* 'Yes', 'No', a 'qualified yes' with need for more discussion, and 'abstain'.

This was not because I could not make up my mind, or happily discovered a good escape hatch; it was much more complicated than that. Simply, I kept on asking myself if there were any questions in religious life renewal—or in life for that matter—which lend themselves to a straight *si* or a *non*. *Abstain* I simply ignored, for that is one level I really find hard to take. But *juxta modum*? Surely, that is life. And I would think that when one has agreed to learn to live in a world, the pattern of its progress being interwoven with the thread of *juxta modum*, one has arrived at a certain level of maturity; for the *juxta modum* vote is saying, if one can so speak: *life is complicated.*

How Christian structures lose their vitality

History has been anything but kind to religious life, for through the course of history it has passed from being a vital, lived Christian experience to being a set of juridical or administrative proceedings.

If you make your way into the old part of the city of Louvain in Belgium you will wander into a series of buildings which have a kind of toytown image: cobbled streets and courtyards and a rather mystical but tremendous silence. You will find the same thing hidden in the city of Liege. Nearly seven hundred years ago, these tiny precincts of peacefulness and silence would have been rife with rumour, for the Council of Vienne in 1312 had spoken rather explicitly about them:

PASSION FOR THE INNER CITY

> We have been told that certain women commonly called Beguines, afflicted by a kind of madness, discuss the Trinity and the divine essence, and express opinions on matters of faith and sacraments contrary to the Catholic faith deceiving many simple people, since these women promise no obedience to anyone and do not renounce their property or profess an approved Rule, they are certainly not Religious although they wear a habit and are associated with such religious orders as they find congenial... We have therefore decided and decreed with the approval of the Council that their way of life is to be permanently forbidden and altogether excluded from the Church of God.[1]

Strong stuff! In fact it would seem that the Council itself felt a modicum of uncertainty, for it finished its highhanded condemnations in the following words:

> In saying this we by no means intend to forbid any faithful women from living as the Lord shall inspire them provided they wish to live a life of penance and to serve God in humility even if they have taken no vow of chastity but live chastely together in their lodgings.[2]

Now, if the problem really was discussions about the Trinity, something could surely have been done about it. But the medieval battles about the nature of religious life were motivated by far too many issues to deal with comprehensively here. At the heart of everything was the tension between *consciousness* and *structure*. There was also the evergreen issue of poverty.

When the crisis of the Beguinages emerged it must be kept in mind that, at least in the Low Countries, men and

LOSING THE INSTITUTIONAL MIND

women were looking at and attempting to understand the developing remoteness of the newer Orders, the Mendicants. Many of the Mendicants were beginning to live comfortably despite their vowed poverty; it was a 'poverty' which at times seemed to suggest that you could have your hundredfold in this world and the next.

This is not too bad when you admit the problem and feel slightly embarrassed by it, but it becomes hypocritical when you attempt to justify it—saying, for example, that you remain 'spiritually detached' from your material possessions. You cannot get away from the fact that there is a marked difference between being 'spiritually detached' from your brand new car, and being on the dole.

In the same milieu and era as the Beguinages, Gerhard Groots founded the Brothers of Deventer. They had their enemies and their friends, and I quote from each. First, the friend:

> In various places many people have started living in common together like clergy in a single house in which they copy books for sale, and those who cannot write, exercise whatever mechanical skills they have, or do other manual work for profit in a neighbouring house. These people work with their hands, and they live on what they can earn by their labours or on their private income. They share everything and seek increase of harmony by having all things in common. They eat together and do not beg. They place one of their number in charge of the house, and they follow his advice and obey him, as pupils obey their master. They follow this mode of life, but principally they hope that by living thus, they will better please God and service him.

PASSION FOR THE INNER CITY

Then the enemy:

> There are persons of both sexes who have assumed the habits
> of a new religious order and hold conventicles. They profess
> no approved rule and they set up superiors for themselves
> at their own pleasure. Under the pretence of devotion they
> draw people to them, doing many things contrary to the truth
> of Holy Scripture and the sacred canons. From the offerings
> of the faithful they build sumptuous houses like regular
> monasteries and within them they practise rites which have
> not been approved by the church.[3]

Centuries later, it would be somewhat difficult to decide
which corner to choose, but there would be no difficulty
in grasping the central issue: it is simply a rejection of the
accepted mode of religious life. Yet at the same time, there
is a desire there for what is at the heart of religious life: to
make a radical choice about where one would place one's
dependencies. This is well summed up in a letter written in
1490 by the Rector of the Brethren at Hildesheim:

> We are not members of an Order, but religious men trying to
> live in the world. If we get a papal order compelling those who
> leave us either to return to us or to enter another order, we
> shall be selling our liberty—that liberty which is the singular
> glory of the Christian religion—to buy chains and prison walls
> in order to fall into line and conform to the religious Orders.
> We, too, will then be subject to servitude, like slaves who can be
> corrected only by punishment. I myself indeed once thought
> that we should accept a Rule and make profession; but Master
> Gabriel Biel corrected me, saying that there were already
> enough members of religious orders. Our way of life springs
> and has always sprung from an inner kernel of devotion. Let
> us not therefore, bring upon ourselves at once the destruction

66

LOSING THE INSTITUTIONAL MIND

> of our good name, our peace, our quiet, our concord, and our charity. Our voluntary life as brethren is very different from the irrevocable necessity of those who live under the rule and status of a religious order. Their monasteries fall into decay through the presence of unstable and undisciplined members, think then how much more our life would be destroyed by the enforced presence of such people.[4]

Obviously such words have very much in mind the problems of the out-of-place religious, but even more than this, one is face-to-face with the most fundamental point of all human dependency, namely, dependency upon other people—in this case a dependency which is based upon a shared simplicity of Christian devotion.

Religious life is above all things an experience, and like all experiences, it is riddled with the tensions and the problems of how such an experience should be contained and maintained with vitality. The age-old question is always present: how to build a structure which will always allow an authentic development of consciousness? Such a question belongs to both the secular and the sacred spheres of human existence.

Fr Hostie[5] and others have analysed, with depth of historical knowledge and sociological precision, the rise and fall of religious life, and have identified five major phases in the life of the religious order. There is the foundation period of about twenty years, bathed in the grace of enthusiasm and charism. This is followed by the expansion period which over a period of fifty years is characterised by institutionalisation. Then there is the onset of the era of stabilisation which spans roughly a

PASSION FOR THE INNER CITY

period of a century or more. Such a period is marked with success, with a sense of well-being and more often than not with an accumulation of property and wealth. At this point, reflection begins to recede into the background. When this happens, dissatisfaction sets in, and there is a frenzied effort to restore things by calling for renewal of commitment. Three choices would seem then to be left to the order: it can become extinct; it can survive on a minimal level for a number of years; or it can find a new life by reading with fortitude the signs of the times, encouraging vision and insight, and making sure that experiment does not abandon the call to pioneer.

The essential problem was suggested in Peter Damian's critique of Cluny.

> When I recall the strict and full daily life of your Abbey I recognise that it is the Holy Spirit that guides you. For you have such a crowded and continuous round of offices such a long time spent in the choir service, that even in the days of midsummer there is scarcely a half an hour to be found, when the brethren can talk together in the cloister.[6]

A Cluniac seconded the motion when he wrote:

> For often before all are seated in the cloister, and before anyone has uttered a word, the bell rings for vespers... After vespers, supper, after supper, the server's meal, office of the dead; after that office, reading of Cassian and so straightway to compline... The members of the brethren have so grown that while they are making the offering of two masses, while the kiss of peace is being given, while one is accusing another

in chapter, while the crowds are being served in the refectory, a large part of the day goes.[7]

God help the poor harassed soul! It was not quite like that for myself in the past, though the ringing of bells summoning us could come with a rather needless frequency. If you had seen reflection upon life as essential to living the full life, you did not get much of a chance in the midst of such a regime.

How structures and institutions create the 'institutional mind'

Structures and institutions are one of the favourite straw men of modern theological and philosophical thinking. It is not a particularly contemporary phobia; it has been around from the first days of Christianity. In light of the above, let me make one thing quite clear: life without institutions and structures is simply unthinkable. Institutions are for my development; they are to assist in my liberation. In the process of liberation and of personal development, if I wish to remain part of a group, certain constraints will need to be accepted. Rahner puts this very well:

> Through our own free choice we create in us and around us customs and institutions that are there to preserve our freedom and rid us of the constraints imposed on us by nature; but what we bring forth in freedom now confronts the free subject as an independent and alienated reality, in fact as a new constraint. And yet the very ambivalent and

dialectical nature of these objectifications should not deceive us; these secondary constraints were created in the first place as concrete expressions of freedom and of ways of helping it to survive.[8]

In the long run, authentic structures are there for the development and fulfilment of my own fullness of life. Schillebeeckx makes the same point when he points out that, among life's values, is

> the value of institutional and structural elements for a truly human life. This is once again a sphere of values which needs concrete norms. On the one hand there can be no permanent life worthy of men without a degree of institutionalisation; personal identity also needs social consensus, needs to be supported by structures and institutions which make possible human freedom and the realisation of values.[9]

However, he also offers a warning, a warning with which we all agree, yet far too often fail to heed:

> Actual structures and institutions which have grown up in history do not have general validity; they are changeable. This gives rise to the specific ethical demand to change them where, as a result of changed circumstances, they enslave and debase men rather than liberate them and give protection.[10]

I believe failure to heed this warning was, and to an extent remains, one of the greatest problems of religious life and the life of ministry. At this point I am not really concerned with the question of institution and structure in itself. I am more concerned with the perception of life, and the orientation of mind, which institutions create. Cone,

LOSING THE INSTITUTIONAL MIND

the author of many works on Black Theology, pinpoints this:

> We see the broad and deep acres of history through a mental grid... through a system of values which is established in our minds before we look out on it... [A]nd it is this grid which decides... what will fall into our field of perception.[11]

Bashing institutions and structures is a fruitless exercise. I went in a good deal for it myself in the past. It is fruitless unless I have already seen the need for personal radical change in my own life, and expressed the willingness to undergo it. All the permutations of structures, and all the criticism of structures, arrive nowhere without my personal readiness to expose myself, in such a way, that I leave myself open to radical change.

I cannot have it both ways. I cannot sleep easy within the bed of institutional certitude and at the same time wish to expose myself to new beginnings. There must be a genuine openness to risk and disturbance of life. I must accept that, if I launch out into the deep, the water may come up to my neck—and that, if it does, I cannot complain. Faith is a leap into darkness, even though my eyes may begin to accustom themselves to the darkness.

When I came to the inner city, I had a desire eventually to speak of new formats of ministry and religious life, but it was the unexpected which took over. I became exposed to an experience which shattered my institutional and structural mind and will. It was not the powerlessness or poverty situation which did this directly; it was the wonder of the human staying alive in the midst of all this. Yet this wonder

PASSION FOR THE INNER CITY

of humanity which faced me also highlighted the sinfulness of a situation which human beings had to face day in day out. In simple terms, having set out to minister to the least of the brethren, the least of the brethren ministered to me.

6

Rediscovering humanity

Beauty in being human ~ The struggle for transcendency ~ Seeing beyond the functional

As I went to work in Liverpool, as I became active, I found myself stopped in my enthusiastic apostolic tracks. I saw people struggling to stay alive in the midst of social neglect, poor housing, bad planning, incongruous education, political manipulation, a repulsive environment, racial discrimination and a vacuous future. But I also found hope in the centre of hopelessness.

I found so many local people and community workers striving to recreate life. I was in the midst of a wounded world, yet I could still hear the heartbeat of God's creation. I was challenged to make sure that I received from this world before I could in any sense act or indeed live with relevancy. Questions exploded in my mind in those very early years: Why did parents, without a sign of hope in the today, stay alive with hope in the tomorrow? Why did community educationalists spend so many hours helping in the maturing of a few children, in a world dominated by a philosophy of success founded upon competitive academic results? Why did these residents, with whom I sat for hours, go on fighting for an adventure playground, and a say over their environment, when experience seemed to suggest their efforts would be fruitless? Where did all this tenderness in neighbourhood care find its origin, in a world of social neglect? Why did they suffer such structural violence, at times being seduced by that violence into violence with each other, when there seemed so little hope in their taking power over destiny into their own hands?

'Being human' needs to be worked at, but one must distinguish between being human from a *static* aspect of life and being human from a *dynamic* aspect. I can speak of the human world, or the world of humanity. In so doing, I point to that whole spectrum of life, filled with the life of humankind, with all its hopes, visions and achievements; but these themselves point to a life of activity, activity which is caught within the intellectual and volitional life of human beings and activity which is the expression of the inner self. The human being, or 'being human' must reflect both the static and the dynamic. I believe Maritain well described what being human means when he struggled with the description of humanism:

> It is impossible to sever the traditions of humanism from the great wisdom of the pagans; we shall at least be on our guard against defining humanism by exclusion of all references to the superhuman and by a denial of all transcendence. Leaving all these points of discussion open, let us say that humanism... essentially tends to render man more truly human and to make his original greatness manifest by causing him to participate in all that can enrich him in nature and history... It at once demands that man make use of all the potentialities he holds within himself, his creative powers and life of reason,

REDISCOVERING HUMANITY

and labour to make the powers of the physical world the instruments of his freedom.[1]

All too often, the phrase 'being human', especially on Christian lips, is put in the context of being weak. It can be complimentary; but it lacks, at least potentially, the urge towards the positive. We have all heard, indeed used, the phrases: 'Well, we're all human', 'God knows you can't be any more than human', and the like. Now it is true enough, when we put the notion of being human within the context of a theology of original sin, that humanity does show a certain tendency to weakness—but being human really has nothing to do with being weak or wanting. To go back to Maritain—I believe he, at least, gives a hint of where the misunderstandings begin. Writing about the difficulty of defining humanism, he says:

> Is it necessary to recall that even to Aristotle it did not come easy? To offer man only what is human is to betray him and to wish him ill: for by the principal part of him which is the mind, man is called to something better than a purely human life ... On this point (if not in their ways of applying it) Romanuja and Epictetus, Nietzsche and St John of the Cross are of one mind.[2]

In other words, being human is being much more than human. It is refusing to be earthbound, and it carries with it the rich and terrible burden of reaching out for transcendency, which is what being human is all about.

75

The struggle for transcendency

As I began my life in the inner city, certain things were uppermost in my mind. I was there to reach for those who were passively and actively alienated from the Christian way of life. I also saw myself getting close to another kind of alienation: that is, the alienation which the poor of this world must face day by day. This latter alienation demanded a change of lifestyle. I saw myself called to create community in the midst of those who were alienated from Christian life. I saw myself very much in the mode of action and giving, even though the act of living a particular lifestyle was important. But the more I looked at this total spectrum of the powerless life of my area, the more I was pushed into the role of a receiver.

I was pushed into this role by seeing the struggle for transcendency, the expression of the deepest qualities which enrich human life, still alive in such a wounded world. This evoked in me two distinct yet inseparable reactions. On the one hand, I began to realise that my search for knowledge and longing for love must begin in a deeper understanding and appreciation of the wonder of God's creation, which remains alive even in those who are named as 'alienated' from the Church. On the other hand, in coming more and more to appreciate this dimension of life, my passion for the powerless, my anger at the oppression, no matter how subtle, which they undergo, began to flare up in my own soul. Thus, for me, the poverty question became much more than just the poverty question.

The power of the powerless to stay alive, with all that is wonderful in human richness, is the message that the Church and Religious Life must first learn about the poverty situation. Yet for us all, the institutional mind still dominates both the perception and the interpretation of that powerless experience. I in no sense relinquish my dreams of celebrating life in this area with those who have enriched me (I mean life celebrated eucharistically), but I do believe a celebration must arise from the richness which is present. To achieve this, I am called to an identification with the poor of this world, and I must discover the priorities both of the human and the divine which are at work in the Church and the world. The beginnings of all this are not to be found in the sociological order, but in the theological order and in the ascetic order. A new 'following' means a new 'denying', and that denying has to do with many of those things which continue to support and perpetuate the institutional mind.

Seeing beyond the functional

My father was a boilermaker and a very devout Catholic. He seemed to me to have been a man who lined up life's priorities fairly well. Some hours before his death he said to me: 'Whatever God condemns me for, he will never be able to say I was a bad boilermaker.' They were words not uttered from the depths of an assimilated theology of the laity; they were not the outcome of theological formation. They were a reflection, a mystical reflection, upon life. They were words without regret, but they were words of ultimate praise.

I am certainly convinced that my father did life's mystical sum very well. You cannot go much further or deeper than relating your committed life as a boilermaker to the ongoing mystery of another life. I am not saying he surrendered his life to a static functionalisation in a capitalistic society, nor do I agree with all that such a philosophy of capitalism stands for. But I recognise that millions find in themselves, from whatever source, the ability to merge the pedestrian struggle of daily life with a hidden mysterious conviction that they are more than this function.

'Travelling on the Underground', writes Gabriel Marcel,

> I often wonder with a kind of dread what can be the inward reality of the life of this or that man employed on the railway—the man who opens the doors, for instance, or the one who punches the tickets. Surely everything both within him and outside of him conspires to identify this man with his functions as worker, as trade union member or as voter, but with his living personality as well. The horrible expression 'time-table' perfectly described his life.[3]

I am sure that Marcel has something of importance to say in this reflection of his with regard to our functionalised world—in his philosophy of existence, he is struggling to see how the functions of life relate to the *mystery* of life. Later, he writes:

> The urgent need for transcendence should never be interpreted as the need to pass beyond all experience whatsoever. For

REDISCOVERING HUMANITY

beyond all experience, there is nothing. I do not merely say nothing that can be thought of, but nothing can be felt.[4]

I believe that people like my father have to create the ground of God's existence out of the raw *stuff* of creation, and that they have to do this in a way which sees no intermediate systematisation of God. For example, liturgy of word and sacrament may be presented to them, and they may be asked to participate in such events in different ways, through an interpretative exercise which is offered to them by a ministering church; but no matter how brilliant and original the interpretation may be, the interpreter is not brought face-to-face with the stuff of creation's daily progress.

My father once hinted at this to me. He evidently sat through a sermon during the depression days, and listened to the priest reminding the congregation about the support of a particular candidate in the forthcoming election who would help to retain Catholic schools. My father remarked that it was a great pity that the priest was protected from worrying about the paltriness of the benefits offered by the Unemployed Assistance Board.

I am sure the priest concerned *did* worry about the people who suffered, but I do believe that God was being subjected to middle-management. The search for knowledge and the longing for love is not bound up intimately enough with a passion for the poor, because that state of the poor is not even open to being experienced. Because of this, I do not believe that I really see creation, and therefore the creator, in a bright nakedness.

PASSION FOR THE INNER CITY

There is a moving meditation of Pope Paul VI which was published on the first anniversary of his death (6 August 1979):

> As for myself, I would like at the end, to have a comprehensive understanding of the world and life, and I think that such an understanding should be expressed in terms of gratitude; everything was given, everything was grace; and how beautiful was the panorama through which it all passed—too beautiful in fact, so that one allowed oneself to be attracted and bewitched by something that was meant as a sign and an invitation. But in any case, one's leave taking it seems, should be one great and simple act of thanksgiving; in spite of its pain, its obscurities, its sufferings and its inexorable transitoriness, this mortal life is something very beautiful, a wonderful reality, endlessly original and moving, something worthy to be celebrated in joy and glory - life the life of man!
>
> Nor is the frame which surrounds man's life less worthy of joyous wonder; this immense, mysterious, magnificent world, this universe with its multitudes of energies, laws, beauties and riches. It is an enchanting panorama of seemingly boundless prodigality. As I look back I am assailed by remorse for the fact that I have not sufficiently appreciated this worldly frame, that I have not given the wonders of nature the astonishing riches of macrocosm and microcosm the attention they desire. Why have I failed sufficiently to study, explore and wonder at the arena in which human life unfolds? What unpardonable indifference, what shameful superficiality! And yet at the end at least I can recognise that his world,.. which was made through him, is stupendous. Yes, I greet you and celebrate you at last with profound admiration and, as I have said, with thanksgiving, for all is gift, behind life, behind nature and universe stands wisdom and with it, I say in this lucid moment of leavetaking (you, O, Christ revealed this to us), stands love.[5]

80

REDISCOVERING HUMANITY

That is a mighty hymn of creation, but it contains with it a note of regret.

I believe Paul VI's moving words are a sign of his laying down institutional and structural preoccupations. This is not to be equated with laying down a love for and responsibility towards the Church; but it is a mental breakthrough, to the stark nakedness of God's creation—which can so easily get entangled with things of little importance to the message of Christ.

From my first night, to all the subsequent days in Ducie Street, I was forced to look at something beyond what I had been used to, 'to see' something beyond what I had been used to. I believe that the 'song of creation' of Paul VI was, in part, the result of not being able to enter into that experience of 'seeing beyond'. I further believe that my father, and many people with whom I 'existed' for the first time that night—and have existed with since—are in fact caught up in that 'object, that experience, which is beyond'.

7

Losing our sense of accomplishment

*He is a white liberal ~ Facing myself, in solitude ~
Activity as a way to avoid the call to suffer ~ Developing
true relationships*

After a short time in the inner city of Liverpool, I was asked to chair a meeting concerned with the allocation of funds to the black community for projects of a particular kind. I was asked because of my work in community development, and because it was thought I would be 'an objective chairman'. It looked like a fairly straightforward exercise.

It turned out to be, however, quite a harrowing experience! The simple fact of the matter was that the black community told the agency allotting the money in general, and me in particular, what we could do with our money. They said, rather forcibly, that money is not the racial problem, and nobody is going to be bought with pieces of silver. Further still, we were told that we were not dealing with an immigrant population (one of the great myths about the Liverpool black population) but a population well over a hundred years old.

82

LOSING OUR SENSE OF ACCOMPLISHMENT

Then one of the activists who was articulating the problem turned on me, and told the audience that I was the most dangerous person in the room: "He is a white liberal," were the words used.

At the time I was hurt, angry and rejected. Afterwards, all kinds of people asked me not to be offended; there was nothing personal in the attack. I went home, and sat in my room and I thought and I prayed. The more I thought, the more I had to ask myself just why I had come into this neighbourhood. What was I about? This marvellous idea, born of thought and prayer, to come to the inner city: what did I want? Above all, what had I really to give? Here am I, unblack, socially accepted and unpoor. I have never gone through the discriminatory suffering which belongs to the black experience. I went cold with the thought that I had dared to articulate, already, the problem of being black. Yet I am part of a deep structural racialism, part of this middle-class, white, postcolonial Britain.

I may not want to be this, but I cannot help but be part of the racist structural psyche. Happy slaves with their kind master were part of my textbooks; *Ol' Man River* and slaves looking out over Jordan was a chunk, and a big enough chunk, of my entertainment. Even my spirituality, with a missionary orientation which lacked a great deal of human sensitivity, had themes of racism. Like it or not, I am part of a structurally racist society. My God, I thought, how am I to be liberated? There is a lot of 'existing with and suffering with' to be faced.

Facing myself, in solitude

I believe the greatest problem of my own life, in the past and to some extent in the present, as a priest and a religious, is my dependency upon making myself relevant by activity. The consequences of this perversion are far reaching. The ministering Church and the religious life far too often underpin a philosophical heresy which is at the roots of Western cultural collapse.

It is the heresy which would equate activity with accomplishment. Priests, religious, social workers, teachers, liturgists, bishops, all of whom may be described as being active, are assumed to be accomplishing things; but we never really see the creation of which we are a part. This manifests itself in the simplistic nature of many of the solutions offered to heal our torn and troubled world. This is not to suggest I am advocating a life of doing nothing; but it is a question of how we do things.

It is a truism, yet one that is worth saying, that I am profoundly responsible for myself. I alone, in a certain sense, can live my life and die my death. Such a statement in no way rejects a philosophy of the communal, but I make this point of the 'aloneness' for a particular purpose. I believe I need to be very careful about avoiding solitude, for solitude and the contemplative life are intricately bound and interwoven together.

I am not thinking of an environmental solitude—it is not the physical desert which concerns me—it is that

LOSING OUR SENSE OF ACCOMPLISHMENT

indefinable land into which I must retreat to face my naked self. The desert is an historical theme of Christian life and a dramatic theme in early Christian asceticism. In this desert, the solitary Christian soul grappled with the beasts and devils of evil. It was a battle, which was meant both to dramatise and bring to notice the battle which needs to be awakened in the depths of myself.

The images were intended to cause me to face myself, and in facing myself to purge all that there is of selfishness. I was meant to watch this battle, and struggle to rid myself of the tendency simply to 'exist with' my *self*—in the sense that I shaped God and man to serve my purposes alone. It was meant to develop within me a consciousness of the need to go beyond myself, to find a union with a 'beyond' which, to use the phrase of Aquinas, many 'call God'. I was meant to be pushed to an inner awareness of myself and in that inner awareness, I was called to a union with transcendent reality.

This consciousness was not to be considered a loss of myself. It was not a question of leaving aside the profundity of human experience; it was meant to be a deepening of myself. Just as by loving a friend, I lose myself in the life of that friend, go out to that friend—yet simultaneously discover the deepest enrichment of my own being. Solitude is linked to this. Solitude in this context is not a state of life; it is a path in life.

In this solitude, I catch the tensions of the world, for I discover the polarities of human existence. The tension to be faced is between living just for myself, or living for the other. Solitude is for a purpose; it is meant to deepen the contemplative side of my life, and to give a clear perception of the meaning of both creator and creation.

In this sense, solitude and contemplation are not merely, if at all, about peacefulness. They are about conflict and tensions. They are not only about the perfection of creation and the work of the good God; they are also about the oppression of that creation, and the work of the oppressor. I may perceive unity, goodness and truth; I must also come face-to-face with discord, evil and falsity. If the inner city has done anything for me, it has made me more and more aware of solitude and contemplation, for I have contemplated the wonder and greatness of the sacred at the heart of this population, and I have contemplated also the oppression and victimisation which it suffers.

Activity as a way to avoid the call to suffer

My first tendency in meeting this, meeting it very superficially and through an 'institutional grid', was to rush for activity. Activity was my greatest dependency in life. I was at home when I was relevantly active, or thought myself to be relevantly active.

Countless spiritual writers have warned Christians against an over-emphasis on *action*. But why? That we may listen in our hearts to the voice of God? Yes, that is one reason. That we may allow the spirit of God to work away, like the whisper or the thunder of Scripture? Yes, that too is a reason. But I would say now in my own life that obsession with action prevents me from *seeing* creation, and therefore

LOSING OUR SENSE OF ACCOMPLISHMENT

from seeing a creator. There is a tiredness in many apostolic lives which no good night's sleep will cure. It cannot cure it because there is this terrible desire to handle, manipulate, put to use and control God and the world. It is the forming operation of life. It prevents receptivity, and ultimately results in little, if any, acknowledging, valuing and admiring this world.

In one dimension *I* do that myself, by being, to some degree, a person of action; but I must also make sure, as an equal priority, that I am *present* by contemplation, as I have chosen to describe contemplation in these pages. My friend is taken into the silent love of my heart—there is our basic union. I can never work for, or act for, or with my friend, without the on-going union in the depths of my spirit. If I am to have communion in friendship, I must see my friend, acknowledge my friend, admire my friend. And my friend is, in a sense, humanity. In particular, my friend is the whole of this community, those close to me day by day and this whole inner city population. Communion means a struggle mutually to share power over destiny. This means much purgation of the self.

In describing the beginnings of the inner city Mission, Nicholas brought me a quotation from Buber, and it said so much to me about my life in the past and what I was missing in the inner city. It was to do with this failure to understand the significance of *seeing*:

> Above and below are bound to one another. The word of him who wishes to speak with men without speaking with God is not fulfilled; but the word of him who wishes to speak with God without speaking with men goes astray.

> There is a tale that a man inspired by God once went out from the creaturely realms into the vast waste. There he wandered till he came to the gates of the mystery. He knocked. From within came the cry: What do you want here? He said, I have proclaimed your praise in the ears of mortals, but they were deaf to me. So I come to you that you yourself may hear and reply. Turn back, came from within. Here is no ear for you, I have sunk my hearing into the deafness of mortals.
>
> True address from God directs man into the place of lived speech, where the voices of the creatures grope past one another, and in their very missing of one another succeed in reaching the eternal partner.[1]

The Passionist inner city Mission was, from its very first moment of existence, founded upon that profound yet most ordinary of all Christian themes, the theme of 'presence'. 'The Word was made flesh', one report in early days began, 'and dwells among us'. The Mission in Liverpool was inspired by that concept. All we have attempted to do is to rediscover ever anew the reality of Christ's presence in our world. This presence of God is a point of permanent return in all Christian reflection. 'The Apostles,' wrote Durrwell, 'speak in concept and preach a doctrine, but what they are bringing to the world is a presence' (The Resurrection, London 1960, 310). Over the years, that theme has deepened for me, but I remember so well walking into a local community and resident meeting in the area, and wondering what I was really doing there. The question kept running through my mind: How am I to be active?

I believe this anxiety over action is one of the more dangerous by-products of the institutional mind. It certainly was the case for me. I believe this to be so because

LOSING OUR SENSE OF ACCOMPLISHMENT

institutions, for the most part, are recognisable essentially by the functions which they fulfil in life. At this stage of my priesthood and religious life—without any sense of bitterness—I believe the priority which has been given to fulfilling a function, instead of being present with our whole selves, is one of the greatest hurdles to be overcome in a radical renewal of religious life and ministry.

Attached to this question of function is a whole series of other questions, which on the one hand prevent a real seeing of this world and of God, on the other, a tendency to stop short of true renewal for fear of disturbing the meaningfulness of what I am.

This is not even to hint at any desire to be rid of priesthood or religious life as visible realities in the world. The problem is, because of the predominance of function, I feel I am establishing relationships in depth, or that I am accepted in my role as witness to transcendency by society—when in fact it is merely my status position which is being accepted. I am part of the furniture of a 'Christian' society. All too often this forces me in certain questions to stand on the side of a 'status quo' philosophy of life.

I must make another qualification here. I firmly believe that theological interpretation of life is a task which demands formation and education and distinctive development personally. However, priesthood, the celebrator of the Eucharist, religious life, the witness to communal endeavour in the development of the Kingdom of God—these must arise from the life of the people in such a way that they are at no time victims of social acceptability. The freedom to be truly prophetic demands a freedom from the norms of social life which define me by status, position and function in society. If I do not face up to this, I am far too often forced into the posture, sincere though it may be, of neutrality. The upshot of all this is that far too much time is spent in preserving the institution—time which should be given in fearlessly facing up to the challenge of developing the glory of creation and resisting the sinfulness of power-plays which destroy that creation.

I find this to be one of the great crises in a tired Western church. Vitality, when it is seen and developed, and when it is real, emerges in those sectors of the church which have really demanded a deep equality: in no way dividing ministry and religious life from the common lot of common man, and more particularly common poor man. It is a question of being able to stop and see *creation*. I believe there is too great a rush towards judging and acting; too little encouragement to stand still and see. When one does not really see, when contemplation does not have priority, I am prevented from entering into the depths of positive suffering. Activity can be the greatest of all escapes from the challenge to suffer.

Let me attempt to extend this theme. The riots of the early 1970s and the early 1980s in the inner city were times when the Church was called to suffer. I believe the Church attempted to do things, and rightly so. I believe that there was more than an attempt. But these were historical moments for depth of contemplation—contemplation not about what we should do, but about how far removed we are from the inner crisis of the urban spirit. Sitting on a wall in Falkner estate in the 1970s and standing outside a centre watching petrol bombs being thrown in the 1980s, on both occasions in the early hours of the morning, I was preoccupied with this thought. Newspapers asked where the clergy were. Some of us were out on the steps of the centres and homes. I wanted reconciliation; I worked for it then, and still work for it now. But I was not part of the suffering reality.

My temptation was either to search for a church role which would affirm the pastoral thesis of the past, or rush to a synthesis which would define a pastoral role in the present. I could not help reflecting that I must learn to live with and understand the whole antithesis in which I stood. The institutions of society had run out of steam, the social, economic and political institutions of society were suffering an energy crisis. A new era was groaning to be brought to birth. This cannot be without suffering, nor without acknowledging that far too much activity and far too much concern with my institutional mind and preservation of the institution has separated me from this torn and tattered world.

Developing true relationships

The God who is revealed to me, as to every creature, in the Christian revelation, is a God of relationships. As this theme of relationships is the definition of the creator, so too is it a definition of creation. Cosmically and personally, the world is held together, and can only develop and progress, by way of profound relationships. Whatever structure or institution humanity creates, it only has value in so far as it prospers such a world of relationships. In all pastoral commitments in life, be they of state or church, there must be activity; but the activity is vacuous without the effort of being committed to the development of relationships. My years in the inner city have brought this home in a painful way. Though a priest and a religious, my forum of activity has been amongst many who have rejected the institutional Church.

It is not a question of presenting the Church to such people for the first time; for them it has been around a long time. The only authentic manner in which I have been able to live my life there, has been in the development of true relationships. I stress the word true, because all too often we use relationships for the sake of an apostolate, whereas it is the actual relationship in itself which counts. I would like to exemplify this.

My companion here, Nicholas, along with a teacher colleague, wrote some time ago about their work in a local comprehensive school. The children they have been given are named as 'problems'. (All too often it is the system which is the problem and not the children). Their writing was centred around the lives of two of the children,

> It is no use beginning any educational venture from where one presumes the pupil should be. Rather it must begin where he actually is. So, with Peter, we had to accept a bitter cynical boy as the starting point. We had to allow him to work through his suspicions of us at his pace and not judge impatiently his various attempts to test our sincerity. We had to put ourselves

LOSING OUR SENSE OF ACCOMPLISHMENT

on trial—a reversal of roles which does not come easily. This client-centred approach may seem obvious, but it is not always seen as the obvious approach in schools.

Yes, it is obvious. But the obvious element is overlooked in too many sectors of what are called 'caring situations'. I know that many ministers of religion would say that relationships with their flock are of supreme importance to them, but we do not always see the sacredness in a relationship—we believe too quickly that in Church terms something has 'to be done' to it. Another example I take is from the pastoral work of a priest in my inner city area, a priest in the parochial setting. In his parish bulletin he wrote:

> I owe a lot to a group of mothers who have been meeting together once a week since the beginning of February. We simply talked to one another and listened to one another about the many experiences of relationship and feelings which are all part of the birth and growth of children. All I could do within this group of thoughtful mothers was to listen and now and again put in a word which could help or rather encourage these mothers to think within their own experiences at a deeper level and see if they could find something sacred, something of God in what they are as parents. We never got around to religion in the sense that I was giving them a sermon! So what happened? A very enriching reflection of life was growing and developing among all of us. Moments of quiet; moments of enlightenment; moments of prayer.

This meeting concerned the first communion of the children of the mothers, but within the relationship established in that grouping, the sacred was really growing

PASSION FOR THE INNER CITY

out of the actual life of motherhood. I do not think it was a question of what should be done to the group, but rather about what should grow from the group. This demands acceptance of the reality of relationship as a sacred experience in itself. In fact it is *seeing* creation.

8

Facing the realities of powerlessness

*Creation and powerlessness ~ Comforting the afflicted,
and afflicting the comfortable ~ How urbanisation
creates powerlessness ~ Church, city, and village vision ~
Collaborating in the struggle*

One rainy night and one particular meeting, for some reason or other, remains fresh in my memory. Perhaps it was the newness of searching which belonged to early days, as we attempted to understand the meaning of our mission, which keeps this memory so much alive. As I walked back from the meeting, certain things I had been searching for began to come home to me. Things began to surface with a certain amount of clarity within my mind. It was not so much the discovery of an answer; it was more the understanding, at a deeper level, of the problem, and the potential of the people with whom I had come to live.

It was a meeting of residents in a sector of the neighbourhood on the borders of our own area. The central issue of the meeting had been the need to create an adventure playground for local children. It had been a stormy meeting, with a great deal of verbal violence. The hut we met in was cold, shabby and unattractive. The seating ranged from infant school desk chairs to discarded armchairs which had long ago surrendered to the weight of humanity. The armchairs had certainly known better environments, if one

PASSION FOR THE INNER CITY

was to judge them by their elaborate design. I remember thinking the powerful must once have sat in them, passing judgement upon the powerless who now sat in them getting angry at the powerful. The verbal violence was a web of accusation and counter-accusation about community workers, some of the individuals present, the schools of the area, the general nature of the environment and the sources and destination of financial resources.

We were all engaged in the illusive urban game of trying to improve our community. There is no time limit to this game, it can go on for decades—it is not unlike snakes and ladders. One week you feel you have really gone up the ladder and power over destiny is in sight, but before you know it, at the next throw of the community meeting dice, you have slithered down the snake back to where you started.

The fact of the matter is, of course, you have no real power. You may have the enthusiasm, the will and the commitment; you feel you have power as well, but you have not really got it. It is firmly lodged elsewhere. It is in the hands of the politician, the bureaucracy with its spin-off institutions and the big business empire with its spin-off financial elite. But that night, and God knows how many nights since, we played our game with great enthusiasm and, as so often happens, not without conflict.

I would not want to be mistaken here. I believe this game must be won by the powerless and I believe it will be won in time. The violence of that and many such meetings, in the powerless sectors of society, is not self-generated; it is provoked from outside. It has its roots in the structures,

FACING THE REALITIES OF POWERLESSNESS

systems and institutions of our world. The distinguished civil servant Morrell more than hinted at this when, in his autobiography, he wrote:

Speaking personally, I find it yearly more difficult to reconcile personal integrity with a role which requires the deliberate suppression of part of what I am. It is this tension and not overwork which brings me, regularly, to the point where I am ready to contemplate leaving a service for which I care very deeply. But the price which the public has to pay is even heavier. For the part of ourselves which we are asked to suppress is the creative part.

There is nothing more individual than an idea. No committee ever has or ever will form an idea. It can only adopt one. Ideas are formed by individuals from the depths of their personalities: they have to be felt before they can be brought to consciousness. And they often have to be sustained over a long period, not infrequently with a modicum of passion, before a process of critical appraisal by others defines their realisation as a valid object of public policy.

I reject the many sneers to which we are subject. But I accept the charge, which is really to say to say the same thing, in different words, that we often seem insensitive to the needs and feelings of the governed, valuing the integrity of our own systems more highly than the integrity of those whose needs we exist to meet.

Shared visions in life must surrender to a structurisation, for it is the structure which will carry them through to a tomorrow. Visions merely born out of a past and created in a present, left to float without any system, turn out to be but visions of today and yesterday. If a vision is to be communicated, it must bow to the process of symbolisation and, indeed, of organisation. Structure makes it possible for a vision to address tomorrow.

Every religious founder has known this. The problem was that the bureaucracy so often born out of the structure which carried the vision, all too often ends up suffocating the spirit which alone can keep the vision alive. The end result of this process, unfortunately, oppresses those who long to share that vision, and does violence to those who are to benefit from that vision, especially in the spheres of caring activities. Nobody is questioning the good intentions and good will. It is quite simply the fact that unreviewed structures all too often end up strangling vision. The beatitudes of Jesus have suffered from such a violence in our speedy structurising hands. The peace which the world cannot give all too quickly becomes merged with the only peace which the world is prepared to offer.

The words of Jesus: 'the poor you have always with you', is not so much a statement of God's plan—it is more a warning that you are always going to have the non-poor with you. Powerlessness, or poverty, and the consequent violence of such situations, are not self-generated. The poor are not, and never have been, a problem; it is the rich who are the problem. An arbitrary and unequal structure of resources is not thought up by the poor of this world. It flows from the decisions of the rich, be they rich by status, position or privilege, or all three. I must not search for the definition of poverty within the so-called cycles of poverty

FACING THE REALITIES OF POWERLESSNESS

and deprivation, rather I must search within the cycle of affluence.

The question I must face now is simply this: what positively was I witnessing in that gathering, that community, and in so many others like them which I have attended? I was existing with, and suffering with, a small community of people wanting to have more, in order to be more. I was in the presence of a profound theological fact and experience. For a religious and priestly vision of the inner city joy and sorrow, it is important for me to start at this point. The theological fact and experience is not because I theologically reflect upon human experience; the human experience is in itself theological, because it is human beings caught up in the process of creation. Before I preach to it, minister to it, liturgically celebrate it or baptise it, I am face-to-face with the revelation of the creation process. Creation is not an event having taken place; it is above all things a process. The infinite reaching of human beings to develop this world and to change it into a true reflection of the unity, truth and goodness of God must be seen at the level of the shabby room and the struggle for an adventure playground. Remember Loew's words in the passage I have quoted:

> And this is where the real social and religious problems are to be met—not in complicated theoretical abstractions, but in the simple questions devolving on lice and such things.[1]

The reality of creation in its glory and the creation which is wounded by personal and institutional sinfulness must be discovered in the prosaic of shabby huts with people who groan in unison with the groaning of creation on its way to glory.

Although I entered a priesthood and religious life which was highly structured, at no point was my infinite potential questioned. I joined an institution which gave birth to a particular style of life. In my early days as a religious, the institutional element was very predominant. I had to submit to many aspects of institutionalisation which were highly oppressive, but because my infinite potential was stressed, the institution fostered within itself, by its philosophy and theology of life, a fundamental truth which would rise up against it when it did attempt to overstate its regulatory role in life. One should not be surprised by the rise of religious against certain forms of institutionalisation—this would apply especially to religious orders of women—when the institution appeared to be going down a road which is oppressive. I say this for a broader reason than any kind of enquiry into religious life or priesthood. It is for this reason:

I am surprised that people are surprised, and especially Christian people, by our riot-torn inner cities. If I confine a person, by category, structure or simply by name, I am inviting violence. The pain which I have come to share with others in the inner city, not that the pain is really suffered by me, is the sense of hopelessness that exists. The people are perceived all too often by others—and this perception must affect them deeply—as a people imprisoned in a particular situation, with No Exit signs present at every turn. I have already referred to the danger of searching for the meaning of poverty within poverty situations themselves. The cause of poverty must be found within the cycle of affluence. The

FACING THE REALITIES OF POWERLESSNESS

sociologist Peter Townsend writes:

> In all societies there is a crucial relationship between the production, distribution and redistribution of resources on the one hand and the creation or sponsorship of style of living on the other. One governs the resources which come to be in the control of individuals and families. The other governs the ordinary conditions and expectations attaching to membership of society the denial or lack of which represents deprivation. The two are in constant interaction and explain at any given moment historically both the level and the extent of poverty...
>
> Different types and amounts of resources provide a foundation for different styles of living. Occupational classes reflect the processes of production, but, since they have unequal resources, they also reflect unequal styles of living. The term styles of living has been preferred to styles of consumption because it suggests a wider and more appropriate set of activities than a term which suggests merely the ingestion of material (and implicitly digestible) goods. There exists a hierarchy of styles of living which reflect differential command over resources...Level of resources reflects the style of living that can be adopted.[2]

What concerns me is that such differences, and the consequent command over access to resources which such differences implies, begets in its turn a 'status quo' philosophy which almost declares: this is the way things are, and this is the way they are to remain. Comments passed after the riots of both the 1970s and the 1980s implied that rioting was caused simply from within the communities where the riots took place. I would say that the cause was from *outside* such communities, and the cause was to be found more in the philosophy and language which the institutions of our society adopted. To lay the blame for riots at the door of parents who cannot control their children, troublemakers and leftists far distant from the riot situation, not to mention other well-worn reasons used, is to fail in really understanding the depth of the problem which an unequal society has caused and fostered.

Comforting the afflicted, and afflicting the comfortable

Above all things, to lay blame in this way is to avoid the fact that society, if it is to survive in peacefulness, unity, truth and goodness, must be submitted to a total revolution in thought and structure. One cannot give the powerless the power over their destiny without the powerful having to face a total change in their own lives, whether they be powerful economically, socially or politically. One cannot have it both ways. One cannot remove the 'contrast experience' with which we are forced to live in our world without radically changing the institutions and styles of life embraced by institutions. One either calls all men and women into an equal creative partnership in the development of God's creation, or one leaves the society open to a permanent cycle of violence.

The violence of language which I have heard used so often has been the shock of my own life—language about the people with whom I exist. They are called 'lay-abouts',

FACING THE REALITIES OF POWERLESSNESS

'scroungers', 'criminals by nature', and even 'scum'. If you build areas of society which are so named, and if you fail at the same time to open up the possibility for authentic equality of opportunity in life, then you invite violence. It is, for example, quite ridiculous to hold to educational equality and at the same time perpetuate any form of privileged education. In Christian circles this is no less than a scandal. For the Christian ethic to allow privilege to exist side by side with deprivation, and even develop a rationale for it, is to run away from the demands of Christ's interpretation of man and woman's partnership with God in the development of creation.

There is a fundamental and radical right within me: 'to be, creatively'. Whatever I have or possess in life, I have and possess in order to be greater in my being, in my 'is-ness'. Our consumer society, which has given priority to the verb *to have*, ends up making life a shoddy experience. Life becomes as plastic as its goods. It contributes to, if I may adapt Heidegger, 'the history of the forgetting of being'. Gabriel Marcel and Erich Fromm, in our times, have spoken prophetically about this theme.

Worse still, the philosophy which gives priority to the verb *to have*, linked in with the values of privilege, status and a general elitism, inevitably leads to the inequality in the exercise of 'having', so that millions of human beings are prevented either from truly being creative or are banished into marginal areas of being creative. The rights of such sectors of society to express what it is to be infinite are suppressed and oppressed. Life's pilgrimage is aborted;

there is no vision of a *terminus ad quem* because the *terminus a quo* is sustained* by a philosophy of life which in effect states: only some shall express their reaching for more of everything and more of everywhere; only some shall live lives bearing witness to the infinite—which is, paradoxically, what the heart of being a finite human person should be. Though he writes as a sociologist, I believe such sentiments underpin Townsend's reflections upon poverty in Britain today:

> What is the social outcome of this unequal structure of resources, and how is it legitimated? Different types and amounts of resources provide a foundation for different styles of living... There exists a hierarchy of styles of living which reflect differential command over resources... [The] level of resources reflects the style of living that can be adopted, as well as social acknowledgement of the worth of the recipients or earners of those resources. Marx put the point graphically: 'Hunger is hunger, but the hunger gratified by cooked meat eaten with a knife and fork is different from that which bolts down raw meat with the aid of hand, nail and tooth.' But society has to foster citizenship and integrate its members, and not merely observe and regulate a hierarchy of life-styles.[3]

One can tolerate the fact that there is this state of inequality, but one finds it hard to tolerate in Christian circles an apologia which would underpin such a state of society. Compassion is simply not enough in this context. There is a crying need for collaboration. I cannot become identified with the poor of this world, but I can at least face

---

* Which is to say, no room for long-term goals because of the pressures of immediate needs.

the challenge of being identified with the struggle of the poor for their liberation. If I accept that challenge, then I must face a radical change in my own life.

The test for the Church is that it must not see the poor of this world as an aspect of apostolate and mission; rather it faces up to the fact that if it is failing the powerless of this world, it is failing the Gospel totally. If we do not face up to the place where sin is felt most in God's creation, then there is little credibility in healing a privileged world. One cannot comfort the afflicted without at the same time afflicting the comfortable. If I do not face up to this demand, I believe I am guilty of a subtle violence against God's creation, a violence far worse than the violence which erupts in a riot-torn city. How I deal with the question of powerlessness is the key to how I deal with the whole of creation.

Urbanisation creates powerlessness

It would take more than a few pages to come to grips with the phenomenon of urbanisation. The reason for this does not rest simply in the fact that we are facing a problem of massive proportions, but there is also a complex cultural problem involved. One cannot overlook, however, the *scale* of the urban problem. We must do this, if only to grasp how many millions are caught in this new cultural net. The pace at which this new phenomenon gathered speed is part of the very nature of the new culture which came to birth. Barbara Ward wrote of this with great clarity:

We have to make the effort of imagination needed to realise that after some fifteen to twenty thousand years of organised human existence in recognisable settlements, the whole character of this habitat is being radically transformed in less than a hundred years. If we take 'urban' as the adjective to qualify settlements of more than 20,000 inhabitants, throughout most of human history at least ninety per cent of the people have lived not in cities but in hamlets, villages or at most small towns.

At the time of the American Revolution, this was the percentage of Americans living in centres of no more than 2,500 people... After a hundred years or so of industrialisation the number of people in urban areas at the end of the nineteenth century was about 250 million in a world population of 1650 million... By 1960, urban population had grown to a thousand million in a world population of three thousand million... Today urban peoples are racing towards the 1,500 million mark out of a total world population of four thousand million . By the year 2000 there will be actually more urban dwellers than rural people in a world population which will have risen to between six and seven thousand million. Bv 1900 there were eleven 'million-cities'... By 1950 seventy five 'million -cities'. By 1985 the million-city will have jumped from 11 to 273 in less than a century.[4]

When we think of this urban development, it is important to remember that we are talking about human beings, and therefore about food, housing, education, communication, health and such factors of human life. The size of the phenomenon and the radical change affecting human life because of it, affect not merely the body of man and woman but the very spirit, the depth of this individual human being. A consciousness of people has not always been uppermost in the powers responsible for the development of the city.

FACING THE REALITIES OF POWERLESSNESS

Barbara Ward's suggestion has not been a priority of such powers:

> But cities must be built not for economics alone—to build up the property market—not for politics alone—to glorify the Prince (in whatever form of government). They must be built for people and *for the poorest first.*[5]

Instead, they have emerged out of a jungle-like struggle of power and greed. Free competition has more often than not been the roots of the phenomenon. In the words of Elaine Morgan:

> Free competition, like a free fight, does not conduce to the advantage of everybody—it conduces to the advantage of the strongest. That is why it has always been popular among nations and groups within those nations, which are economically in the healthiest state at any given time.[6]

Nowadays, some of the sentiments of the Mendicant preachers of the 13th and 14th centuries—as they enthusiastically roamed the world with their new apostolic methods and approaches—turn a little sour. Either they were somewhat naive, or after their own material good, or they felt by putting a lot of people in one place it was an easier and quicker way of saving souls en masse.

They were in at the curtain raising, from a Church angle, of the urban phenomenon. Dr Little's book *Religious Poverty and the Profit Economy in Medieval Europe* lists some of the rather optimistic views, held by distinguished men, about the potentiality of the City. His reference to St Albert the Great will suffice to illustrate this tendency. The distinguished doctor of the Church was preaching a series of sermons at Augsburg, around the year 1220. The title of the series was, 'A city upon a hill cannot be hidden'. Albert, having stressed the need for virtue in the lives of the rulers and city fathers, also suggests that a city will get nowhere without riches. One reason he gives for this need for priority of the rich is their power to defend the city.

> We see this in many cities, that some who are powerful and rich are able to maintain a thousand men in time of war.[7]

The trouble is the seeds of oppression are forever found, in a very special way, in the consecration of an elite, be the elite political, corporate, or military. Some sixty years later another friar, having admired and wondered at the glory of the city of Milan, put his finger on a very practical problem, and a very modern one at that:

> After what has been said, it is evident that in our city, life is wonderful for those who have enough money.[8]

These words of the Milanese friar would get more than one knowing nod of assent from any contemporary urban population. In fact, in my own area his sentiments would be accepted with a good degree of excitement. We may feel more inclined to talk about 'higher things', but in the urban scene of today, to be without money puts one in the position of having little inclination for higher things. The struggle with the price of butter, bread, jam and baked beans is a rather relevant struggle. It is a struggle linked to

FACING THE REALITIES OF POWERLESSNESS

survival. Assurances that some financial and political elite are getting the books right helps little, if at all, to offset the stigmatisation and alienation which take over vast sectors of a population. As dole queues become longer and longer, it is the human spirit which is under siege.

Such factors and signs are but the characteristics of powerlessness in the city. Too often we are inclined to define urban areas of deprivation (this applies especially to the inner city situations) by lining up the characteristics of social malaise. It is so important to keep in mind that one defines nothing in life without searching for causality. When one comes then to the urban mess of our times one must face up to what has caused it in the past and perpetuates it into the present. As T.L. Blair has written:

> There is a crisis of human identity in cities, and the illness lies somewhere down in the urbanised society itself, inside its value conflicts, its exploitative social institutions, and its alienated individuals.[9]

I would add to Blair's description the words 'alienated groups and classes'. Who is responsible for this infectious illness? Who is the source of false values which lead to conflict? Who is the exploiter? Who creates exploitative institutions? Who alienates? It is certainly not the powerless of this world. The powerless need a fearless critic and an uncompromising collaborator, but such a critic and collaborator needs first to hear and feel the articulation of the powerless.

Church, city, and village vision

One often wonders if the Church in its organisation, and indeed in its mentality, is still affected by a rather village vision. R.W. Southern hints at this:

> Despite all the natural disorders and disruptions which afflicted the countryside it was possible to treat the rural community as a stable and inert mass amenable to organisation and control. But what has to be made of the towns—anarchic, engaged in pursuits doubtfully permissible in canon law, embracing extremes of wealth and destitution, subject to over-employment and unemployment different from anything known to the rural community? To such a society the ecclesiastical organisation had not yet, and perhaps never has, adapted itself.[10]

I believe one should be careful about believing that this 'adaptation' or 'strategy' is to be found essentially in the sphere of structure, organisation or system. Such an approach is too institutional, and too quickly becomes geared to 'action' in general and what one may call 'apostolic activity' in particular. Some years ago, the Jesuit Daniel Berrigan wrote:

> Look, we still can offer something, and we invite you to follow; this is the direction and these are the tactics that brought us where we are; and to be where we are is humanly valuable. There's nobody who can talk that way. There are either theorists of religion or theorists of politics or theorists of this and that, but there are very few whose lives are planted where human life is in the breach.

FACING THE REALITIES OF POWERLESSNESS

What occupies my own mind in the inner city, what has been almost a conversion experience for me, is the need to stand still where human life is in the breach. Such a standing still is not an aimless kind; it is not a careless hanging around. It is the standing still, the standing erect, near the experiences of suffering, pain, joy and wonder, revealed in the lives of a people, for the sake of closer union with them. It is a contemplative reality. One suffers moments of terrible aridity and moments of great productivity. Half-light encompasses you and you know not whether it is the dawn or the twilight. The violence of Golgotha's 'I thirst' and the gentleness of Galilee's 'He is risen', quickly exchange places in your soul. A fellow Passionist, Stanislaus Breton, described this 'standing still' in an address to the International Synod of the Passionists:

> What are the operations which correspond to the proposition: I believe the Cross of Christ, Salvation of the world? At the risk of surprising you, I will address this proposition by speaking of an operation which does nothing beyond itself and which can therefore be called, according to the American mathematician John Yarnelle, 'the indifferent element'. By designating this operation as 'indifferent' it does not mean that it can be neglected. Far from it. Rather, it is called this precisely because, added to every other apostolic operation or work, it does not change it at all in as much as it makes it possible and necessary in depth. In this regard let me give an easily understood explanation. Everyone knows that in arithmetic zero added to any other number does not change that number.
>
> This means that the 'indifferent element', although it does not do anything, is nonetheless the most indispensable

PASSION FOR THE INNER CITY

element because, according to the way we conceive it, it conditions the very possibility of arithmetic. So likewise the operation of which I am speaking and which does nothing, which in this sense is the spiritual and mystical equivalent of the mathematical zero, is the most indispensable of operations. It is that without which we would be, according to the apostle Paul, only cymbals more or less sounding.

I see the symbol of this operation in the attitude of the Virgin in St John's gospel. 'By the Cross stood his mother'. She stood erect near the cross. To stand erect near is an operation which undoubtedly does not accomplish anything great but which still decides everything in depth. She stood erect near the cross is exactly the same as was, in another context, the word of the Johannine prologue where the word was 'with God'. He was thus with God before the world was and was the reason the world became possible as the result of authentic creation.[11]

As I have already explained, my own obliviousness to the wonder of 'being'—an obliviousness caused by an obsession with, or dependency upon, activity—is one of my own purgation points in the inner city of Liverpool. This obsession seduced me away from really seeing 'the being of humanity'. Thus this theme of 'existing with and suffering with', is not a vacuous idling around the edge of humanity in its suffering and resurrection. On the contrary it is an integral part of a contemplative activity which is destined towards a more profound act of union which, in its turn, will produce a more real life of action.

It may be of help to draw briefly upon an analogy here. Christian contemplation aims ultimately at a perfect union

FACING THE REALITIES OF POWERLESSNESS

with God: 'perfect' according to the conditions of living in this world. The contemplative, therefore, is forever struggling for a 'with-ness' in regard to the implicit and explicit godly realities of creation. And more explicitly the contemplative is struggling for a 'withness' related to the mind of Christ which reveals the meaning of God.

To philosophise belongs to the order of contemplation. One of the major tasks of philosophising is the elucidation and clarification of existence itself, and a 'withness' in some form, is wholly necessary. In other words, being able to describe and discuss 'existence', depends upon me being vitally 'with' what is existing. Surely, no matter how subjective it may be, the poet and the artist in their communication are dependent upon an 'existence with and suffering with' the 'other'. Such an *existence with and suffering with* doesn't necessarily result in anything—thus we are inclined to overlook it in our analysis of life—yet nothing is done without it.

Thus the 'existence with and suffering with', which is my adaptation of Breton's use of the indifferent element, is not only necessary for asceticism; it is a necessary cause for any action which must take place. Without such causality there can be little worthwhile action. In this sense the contemplation and the action are permanently interwoven. What I have seen, or what I have been brought to see, is not some prosaic process of people living out their lives. I can implicitly express what I have seen by taking to heart the words of Paul VI:

PASSION FOR THE INNER CITY

As I look back I am assailed by remorse for the fact that I have not sufficiently appreciated this wordly frame, that I have not given the wonders of nature, the astonishing riches of macrocosm and microcosm, the attention they deserve.

But deeper still, I believe, no matter how imperfectly I may have achieved it, because of being forced to see the wonder of the people of the inner city, I have been brought deeper into an understanding of the sinfulness of powerlessness.

Redemptive activity, no matter what apostolic forms it may take to itself, is useless without seeing the wonder of the creation process which is all around me. The radical demand of Christian living is to celebrate the whole of creation. This celebration of the whole of creation is about giving meaning to life and death. It must give birth, as it must be born from, a passion for knowledge and a passion for love and to be loved. Such a celebration, if it is really and truly exposed in its seeing to creation, will experience also the meaning of the crucified God. A passion for the powerless will be evoked when the cry of the poor is heard, for such a celebration will come face-to-face with a wounded world today.

There is enough at the heart of our urbanised world to evoke all of Russell's three passions, but a priesthood and a religious life must stand still to see that creation. I find that I have been pushed to the limit to stop, to see, to stand near in respectful awe and openness before that creation in the inner city.

Collaborating in the struggle

I should make it very clear that in addressing these questions to a Church, I am addressing them to myself, and they are questions which I find very hard to face. But I believe they belong to a critical theme in contemporary society. The gulf between rich and poor, between affluent and deprived, between powerful and powerless, increases. It is a worldwide phenomenon. For the Christian, it is critical historically because it means that the numbers of those who are excluded from the process of developing God's creation increases day by day. The danger, I believe, is to attempt to meet this crisis by a search for relevant activity, but there is also a more positive aspect to the crisis. There is a call to rediscover a theology, an interpretation of God's word revealed to us, by beginning our reflection more in anxiety about the future of God's creation, and the infinite longing and yearning which is at the heart of that creation, than in an anxiety about certain structural crises which face the Church of today.

This is not to say that structure is of no concern, but one should encourage a new consciousness, fed upon the plight of the powerless, which will in its turn dictate, in part, the kind of structure we wish the Church to be. It is calling us away from any form of mere experimentation with things which we feel to be more up-to-date, and directing us onto the path of pioneering a new Church in a tragic yet glorious world.

There are, if I may so put it, three breads to be broken on the table of the world. Those three breads can be discovered in St. John's gospel in the sixth chapter. There is the bread which feeds the hungry; the bread of intellectual enrichment; and the bread of the Eucharist. The breaking of each bread is mutually dependent upon the breaking of the other two, for celebration exists in the breaking of all those breads. One cannot compassionately feed the hungry unless one builds structures in our world which allow the same hungry to reach for infinity. Neither body or mind must experience oppression.

In the same way, one cannot teach any man or woman to reach for infinity, and therefore have power over destiny, unless one collaborates with them in a struggle for material resources so that nobody goes hungry. The breaking of the bread of the Eucharist is the final celebration of communion with each other in God. It is centred upon the one who welcomed into fulfilment those who had responded to him, revealed hungry, in prison, sick, naked and homeless, in the least of the brethren. In the mystery of Jesus, the Eucharist brings all of us home to God and to each other.

I have gone on marches in the inner city; I have fought for better housing; I have been part of the struggle for better education for our children; I have stood on the street in riots; I have been part and parcel of the struggle for community power; I have set my face against my own racism and the racism of others. Why, I have often asked myself, have I done these things and will continue to do these things? Because I believe where creation is sinned against, where human beings suffer, Jesus is crucified; because I believe

FACING THE REALITIES OF POWERLESSNESS

where causes are won for authentic freedom and power over destiny in the work of creation, Jesus rises again. How I have done this in the inner city is another question, yet it is the most important question of all. I have done this because I have not been alone. I have done this because I feel one of the richest experiences of my ten years has been my grasping, to some degree, the profundity of 'existing with and suffering with'.

9

Losing our dependencies

What are you to depend on, in life? ~ Calling old dependencies into question ~ Launching out with faith into the unknown

I said that the General Chapter of my order in 1968 was an extraordinary one: an era of renewal, even if we didn't yet know what shape it would take. One thing is certain, though: in that era of change, a lot of people were deeply hurt. It has been said that in the middle of a revolution someone has to be hurt. My problem is, we pretended it was a revolution—in fact, we did little more than shift around the furniture. I do not say this in a silly critical sense—you see, I was part of it, and enthusiastically so.

I am being wise after the event, but I do not think we really faced the fundamental problem of *what* we were building our renewed principles on.

One of the first acts of our Chapter was to leave an opened copy of the New Testament out in the assembly hall—a public 'enthronement' of the Gospels, making a statement about returning to fundamental Gospel principles.* One

—

* One of the major themes of post-Vatican ecclesial renewal was the invocation of the principle of evangelism. By this I mean the desire for, and encouragement towards, the principle of the Gospel in its simplicity.

group also demanded that an open copy of an early edition of the rule of St Paul of the Cross should likewise be enthroned; others had a strong reaction against this.

Within the dispute, there lay concealed a great deal of fear and a great deal of hope; there were seeds of dissent as to how far we should move bravely into a new era, and how far we should affirm the past; but underneath everything was the wish to declare where one's dependencies were to be in the future of the order, and indeed, in life in general.

If this seems to be a mere kitchen debate of a relatively small religious order, I would argue that this is basically the root question of the total Christian community. General and international groupings of this kind cannot be simplified too neatly in their disputes, but I believe the question: *What are you to depend on in life?*, was writ large and can, in the idiomatic sense, be understood all too often as the writing on the wall.

I have already referred to Prior Richard, who left St Mary's Abbey to found Fountains Abbey. When the Abbot of St Mary's interviewed Richard and his companions, his appeal to them to give up the Fountains venture completely missed the very point of the dispute. Richard begged the Abbot to help him, but the Abbot replied that the loss of so many of his leading assistants would be a serious loss to him, and that he and the rest of the community wished simply to live by the customs that were traditional to them. That was the very point. Richard and the others could see no road forward for them in life within the framework of that traditional customary situation. To develop their lives, such a dependency simply would not do; they had to seek another one.

It is my set of dependencies in life which the powerless of this world finally call into question. The dependencies which I decide upon, develop and protect in my life are, for the most part, a mirror in which I see my life reflected; they reveal the very nature of my Christian life. Question my dependencies in life, and you question my life.

Calling old dependencies into question

There is a metaphysical and a revealed theological sense in which I am totally dependent upon God; but I only come to understand the *meaning* of my dependence upon God insomuch as I experience myself as a free human being, a being with responsible choices to make for my own fulfilment. Dependency on God means seeking to make choices in life which one believes are for the development of a world in which the transcendent oneness, goodness and truthfulness of God are made more manifest.

Implied in this is the fact that I will, and indeed must, declare dependencies upon many other things. All other dependencies are interwoven into my dependency upon God, and they will differ between all of us. German soldiers singing Silent Night, and German Jews shivering in neighbouring huts at the thought of the gas chamber, cannot but produce different philosophies of divine dependency. A priest working in the middle of the inner city, and the inner city child whose situation commits them to a life of

LOSING OUR DEPENDENCIES

powerlessness, may have the inner city in common—but the way in which they have dependency upon God is bound to have its differences. I may say I am dependent on God, but that means I must state how that is so, and this demands that I declare myself to others.

To be an official card carrying member of the accepted religious life in the Church demands that I accept dependencies. One of these, in contemporary religious life, is the wider faith community. This can sometimes have its drawbacks—the case of Don Bosco is revealing.* His was one of the most revolutionary of the new foundations, but Bosco had to rewrite his rule several times before it satisfied authorities that new initiatives would still conform to the approved formulae of a by-gone age. Such agencies can sometimes distract any group of religious from really getting down to what are to be their fundamental dependencies in life.†

Those days of the Renewal Chapter were wonderful days: friendships were made, love was stated and hopes were born. I refuse to disown such memories; still less do I countenance cynicism about them. If they did not live up to their hopes entirely, I believe the reasons rest in complicated patterns

---

* John Bosco (1815-1888) founded the Salesians in Turin, Italy, known for their work helping poor children during the Industrial Revolution, and pioneering 'preventive', care-based approaches with juvenile delinquents.

† Such a tension has deep roots, going back to the Fathers of the Desert, the beginning of all monastic life experience. One of them remarked that a good monk should avoid women and bishops! Such a composite could not possibly be seconded today, whatever way you wish to distinguish it.

PASSION FOR THE INNER CITY

of human thoughts and actions, and a fear of insecurity, but much was achieved by a struggling brotherhood.*

At times I think there was a rather self-conscious search for superficial relevancy. I remember so well the decision to write a document about 'Social Concerns'. I was one of those who sat through the night writing this document, but what we did was quite hilarious, in spite of the sincerity of the moment. We simply listed all the problems of the world, from the Bomb to Northern Ireland, and stated that we were deeply concerned about each one of them. This anxiety about relevancy truly haunted many of us and the words 'bringing up-to-date' were frequently uttered. I think this often led us into an exercise in cosmetics rather than to the need for major surgery.

There were other issues which prevented self-examination at any depth. This was to be expected in a gathering of men from every part of the world attempting to draft a charter of life for the future, which would truly honour the past, realistically interpret the present and tentatively look into the future. Such issues caused hard dispute. I will mention just three of them.

Firstly, there was this belief that if you prayed harder, and kept the rule better, all would be well, and renewal would be realised. It is what I may call 'the principle of

—

* Our Chapter in 1968 ultimately produced a charter which could be looked upon with pride; in terms of 'rules', it was, and remains, a magnificent document, and I have seen few better come from the other orders in those years. However, looking back, I feel that principles were gathered more from religious life as a *phenomenon* than from religious life as an *experience* and, more troubling, perhaps no experience *outside* religious life at all.

LOSING OUR DEPENDENCIES

intensification': be and do what you have been and done in the past, and all will be well—as long as you choose to be better, and act accordingly.

Secondly, there was a kind of uneasiness as to what the wider Catholic community would say about what we had written, or were attempting to write. Accountability was measured more by what was expected of us by a higher body, rather than by our own insights.

Finally, as in all institutions, too often the sense of nostalgia took over from the authenticity of memory. All of this is understandable, and must not be too harshly criticised. But I think such issues prevented us from facing up to what the realistic dependencies of a religious order should be, at the end of the twentieth century.

However, within the theology of my own order—in its central demands—there was something which, if interpreted in the light of new or restated dependencies, would go to the heart of the world in which we were living. I speak, of course, of the Passion of Jesus: my order is built upon that historic moment in the life of the Word-made-flesh, which spells out dramatically the experiences of powerlessness.

If anything demands of you a review of your dependencies in life, it is this revelation of the powerlessness of Jesus, both as an historic event, and as revealed in the powerless of this world. To get to this, you must agree 'to exist with and suffer with' the powerless of this world in some real way. If you do, you will be forced into a reflectivity which, in turn, forces you to ask where your dependencies are to be in life.

PASSION FOR THE INNER CITY

I am sure that I did not see it like that in those days; therefore, if what I write is seen as judgemental, I must make it clear that I put myself on trial. I am attempting to say something, in the light of my own experience within a religious order, about post-Vatican II religious life, and priesthood in particular—and, by implication, about the Christian community in general. Obviously there is room for many qualifications, for much good came from those days, and much good is being achieved today.*

I said that our new era of thinking brought about a great deal of disturbance and hurt in the lives of many religious and priests; but I believe this disturbance rested more in the world of their chosen and inherited dependencies than in their theologies. To be sure, it was a theology which created those dependencies, but in the concrete situation the actual and potential trauma and hurt were to be located in their dependencies. There was, and still is, a great deal of hurt involved, and one should not be too cavalier about this. One is given a set of symbols, systems or structures, which guide, enclose and protect my life—and if they are taken away or even belittled, one is called into or pushed into a 'waste land'.

The religious habit; times set aside for prayer; forms of address; sources which possessed the force of the authoritative voice of God at all times; age-old liturgical

—

* As I explained at the start of the book, it was during the General Chapter that the seed of the Passionist inner city Mission in Liverpool was planted— that project which is my life today. The things I am thinking about now are a combination of my experiences in the inner city and my reflections upon religious life, priesthood and the Church.

LOSING OUR DEPENDENCIES

expressions of approach to God—these were some of the dependencies which were called into question, and sometimes with a measure of insensitivity. I believe I was part of that insensitivity; perhaps I still am. The difficulty is marrying principle and conviction with thoughtfulness and charity.

Launching out with faith into the unknown

As I look back, and even look at, what is sometimes called the process of updating the Church, I am not altogether swept off my feet with enthusiasm. Bertrand Russell once wrote, in a letter to Gilbert Murray:

> What first turned me away from utilitarianism was the persuasion that I myself ought to pursue philosophy, although I had (and have still) no doubt that by doing economics and the theory of politics I could add more to human happiness. It appeared to me that the dignity of which human existence is capable is not attainable by devotion to the mechanisms of life, and that unless the contemplation of eternal things is preserved, mankind will become no better than well-fed pigs.[1]

I believe in all our lives the philosophy of utilitarianism is forever sneaking in—perhaps often enough invited in. It's the habit of choosing what is useful, and perhaps seems very contemporary, but deep down does not disturb me radically. I would suggest that this has been a particularly critical problem for the Church. I can simply select what is useful from a modern era, and yet never really come to grips with the broader issues which will seriously question me or the institution behind which I can hide.

There have been new modes of liturgy; new ways of doing things have been encouraged; new forms of linguistics have been adopted. There was, and is, a growing use of the content and methods of community development; there is an effort to do things in a different way. But it is very selective, and often avoids the deeper questions which lead to a certain radical renewal of religious life and ministry.

Jack Dominian pointed to a more radical challenge when he wrote:

> Man's involvement with God must take place at a level of engagement of the mind and the psyche which is appropriate for a society which has immense opportunities of unravelling deeper layers of the image of God in man. That is why simplistic religious crusades just do not work. Man's spiritual longing is as strong as ever, but the level of engagement between man and God must reflect the realisation of these new depths in our humanity which social, psychological and scientific horizons have opened up. One aspect of the spiritual crisis of the age is the inability of the Churches to engage man accurately at a deeper level of existential experience which will do justice to these newly opened horizons.[2]

Dr Dominian points to the positive side of the picture. He is calling the Churches to face a new world with 'radical astonishment', to use Heidegger's phrase. Simultaneously, however, so much has emerged, and has been encouraged to emerge, which oppresses these immense opportunities in the lives of millions. Man does not want to be one of Russell's

LOSING OUR DEPENDENCIES

'well-fed pigs'. The reaching for, and the expression of, the 'eternal things' remains firm and sure. The problem is how the Church, in collaboration with others, is to create the true context and, when accepted, the authentic articulation of eternal roots and longings. My question now is: In my search for God and my understanding of the mystery of Jesus, upon what must I depend?

I have settled for the belief that an understanding of 'to exist with and suffer with' will lead me to new dependencies, because I believe that I will grow in a deeper understanding of creation, and so rediscover the meaning of redemption or the 'new creation'. I will begin to see that, without collaboration with all men and women of good will in the development of creation, there is little sense or use in resting in the stance of compassion.

'Becoming' becomes an exciting possibility, and avoids the sterility of that interpretation of 'being' which highlights an arid stability which leads to the burial of creativity; consciousness I know will envelop me, and no structure can be so secure as to oppress that rise of consciousness. I will be called into a world of pioneering as a daily experience, which means launching out with faith into the unknown. Thus I will be prevented from simply paddling in the experience of the experimental which, wonderful as it is, seems to excuse me from that certain finality of commitment which is at the heart of the Jesus invitation to deny the self and follow him. This I shall do because 'to exist with and suffer with' means grasping with both hands the experience and the fact of community, which, when fully understood, leads me to the centre of the city of God and the city of Man.

PASSION FOR THE INNER CITY

Man is communal, and God is communal, and struggling with the communal means struggling with the revelation of human anew through God and God anew through humanity. Though the new creation depends upon revelation, revelation is void if it attempts to be stated outside of the reality and the experience of the relational. There must always be 'the others' and 'the Other'.

10

The realities of a new community

Community is the epiphany of creation ~ A society which forces people to wait ~ The cry of the poor is a summons to change our lives radically

Community is the epiphany of creation. It is the epiphany always longed for, very often struggled for and sometimes gloriously realised. Its potential exists at the very central point of creation: it is brought to actuality when humankind mutually strive for equality of relationships, and respectfully treat and develop the physical world in which it exists.

Community, like all profound realities, lies open to trivialisation. This should never be the case for the Christian. For in the web of relationships is to be found the hint, at least, of transcendency. The God I know and have heard about, in the words of Jesus, is the God of relationships. When creation is described as groaning for redemption, the groan will turn into a hymn of praise only when the harmony of relationships is realised—as it is from time to time, though with an exiled imperfection. The ethic of Jesus was fundamentally about this harmony, for in essence the ethic of Jesus was about a life of total equality amongst all human beings. It was about a shared power, shared in order to be creative, in which creativity would be found the authentic expression and exercise of freedom.

PASSION FOR THE INNER CITY

Personal and structural selfishness is always waiting to ambush those who would attempt such a vision. Even the best of lives, even those wrapped up in the noblest of vocations, contain degrading dependencies which make a mock of true community. They therefore mock and abort the plan of God's creative will. Status, position, economic security, political manipulation, parading in the robes of power, longing to be honoured in the market place—these are some of the values which lead to corruption of that shared power which rests at the heart of God's creation. 'To exist with and suffer with' is ultimately about sharing of power over the whole spectrum of life.

I would think that if incarnational theology has anything to say, it is surely about how, paradoxically, the more one becomes godly, the more one becomes truly human. The equation of transcendence and immanence works itself out into a solution which honours both elements. God may well be able to talk about himself, but I suggest that one can only talk about the reality of God because one talks about the reality of man and woman. I am not saying that God is an invention of man, but that the only way I can talk about God is by talking about his relationships with humanity and the web of relationships which holds humanity together. I only talk about the creative power of God to get to the point of understanding the profound right of every human being to be creative too. I cannot talk about God without being conscious of man, and if I attempt to forget God, I cut the human spirit from its moorings. There is no other arena in which we can search for and understand how to define God except the human arena in which we find ourselves.

THE REALITIES OF A NEW COMMUNITY

If human beings attempt to escape from each other, then they escape from God. One cannot discover God in a total wilderness of our own making. We are born to exist with each other, and if this is so, we must agree to suffer with each other. If we attempt to achieve this, then life's pilgrimage is about sharing power over creation, as it is materially and spiritually revealed to us day by day. If I refuse this path, then I choose to exist with myself, which is, at least, the beginnings of sinfulness. If the Gospel calls us to anything, I believe it calls us to a new translation of the reality and experience of power. This is the conversion point. God and the world are not mine, they are essentially ours.

Anything which gets in the way of that shared possession destroys both the meaning of God and the meaning of being human. I would think it quite pointless to attempt to unravel the meaning of the crucified God, and simultaneously rest content with philosophies and structures which run counter to the search and struggle for a world without privilege, status and position.

One cannot permit oneself to 'put up' with inequality. This is not a political philosophy nor an economic plan nor a social vision. It is at the very heart of Christian revelation and, therefore, at the heart of all that is truly human. Unity, truth, justice and love are not aspects of living, they are the stuff of living. One cannot give God a chance unless one really gives humanity a chance. I shall never know the meaning of grace if I am not respectfully gracious in the presence of every human being.

Some years ago Brian Wicker wrote:

> The protests which I have discussed ... offer us some conception of the kind of visionary ideal to which a sensitive Christian can, and (I suggest) ought to, commit himself. But the immediate impracticability in the face of contemporary pressures seems nevertheless all too evident. The danger, in this predicament, as I have said, is to abandon the vision which the literature of protest embodies, and to fall back on contentment with merely ameliorative, practical measures.[1]

I believe this shared power over life, which I see as the central point in a philosophy and theology of community, is day by day reasoned away by the philosophy of impracticability. However, in my own life, my Passionist community have brought me back to—even presented for the first time—this vision of life: the people of my own area, many religious, priest and lay friends who long for a new Church of the poor, the many community workers and activists along with other professions in my area, Christian and non-Christian. I believe this to have been the case because, all at differing levels and in differing degrees, we have in some way surrendered power over life to each other. In so doing, we have touched the sacred at its deepest level in life. There has been a great sense of 'existing with and suffering with', but what has happened at this point in my life has turned my mind to a deeper sense of the need for greater *kenosis**. Looking into my area, looking specifically

---

* The act of 'self-emptying, and becoming fully receptive to God's will.

THE REALITIES OF A NEW COMMUNITY

at the work with young people initiated by one member of my community, the question does relentlessly emerge: To what degree does one go, how far does one go, in giving power over my life to the powerless youngster?

Rational arguments can so easily distract from the major issue. When the work of that companion religious needed more space, I must say that I found all kinds of reasons why I should not surrender my own room. I came in one day and thought to myself how ridiculous such rationalisation is. It was not as if there was nowhere for me to live. In fact I now live in a basement flat, with another member of the community, in a house occupied by seven old people who have spent most of their lives in mental institutions. That flat was a possibility during the whole debate about whether I should move. The community gathers each day in the flat, and it has become the base for all our dialogue and life. But what is a room in a house, in terms of personal value, when put beside the needs of a young inner city population with nowhere to go? If one child has the possibility of discovering his or her creativity more easily through the space vacated by me, what is it, deep down, which still forces me into vast rationalisations? In the last analysis it is nothing more or less than that desire to 'exist with' the self, to preserve the self, to persuade the self of needs, needs which are merely the outcome of past patterns of life and action.

I look at these issues day by day: the homelessness; the lack of social acceptability; the racial discrimination; the total inability to invest in a future; the painful steps which must be taken just to walk one mile; the increasing incursion into life of the non-compassionate society. These issues make me really wonder about so many matters which seem to preoccupy the Church towards the end of the twentieth century. That overall pre-occupation conditions me, as a middle-aged religious and priest, to fall into the trap of tentativeness. The grandeur and squalor of the inner city have liberated me, and my commitment is deeper now than it was on the day of my religious profession and priestly ordination, but should I be so bored and weary with so many ecclesiastical things? Perhaps boredom is even the wrong word—I am tempted by the word irrelevant, but I do not have the right to pass judgement on people. Suffice it to say that I cannot summon up the energy to face many of the questions which seem to be so crucial in ecclesiastical circles. I find it hard to summon up the energy not because I want to run from theological or philosophical reflection— far from it—but the questions seem so far removed from a wounded world.

A society which forces people to wait

Most of my waiting in life has been of a luxurious kind. I mean most of the things I have waited for I knew could, and even would, eventually turn up. But there is a kind of waiting which I have never really had to face in any kind of depth. I have never had to wait for something, and something absolutely essential to my person as a human being, knowing in my heart of hearts my waiting was purposeless. To be creatively human, and humanly creative, I have never had to wait on the good pleasure and the kind services of another human being. I have never had to say to

THE REALITIES OF A NEW COMMUNITY

myself, I will be what I want to be *when* that other person or those other persons radically change their lives.

It is true that great artists and, indeed, the great mystics, have all experienced the pain of waiting, but they knew that it was part of the process necessary to final fulfilment. Their waiting was biblical—I mean, there was in the People of God an assurance that God would come. It was hard to wait for the day, but the strength of the authority left no doubt in their minds that He would one day be amongst them. Therefore, their very time of waiting could be turned into a process of preparation; it could have the gentle and inspiring themes of joy and expectancy in it. In the words of one of my Passionist brethren, Carroll Stuhmueller: 'The motif of waiting ... nurtures that type of faith essential for contemplative prayer... Waiting can be as joyful as a child's expectation of birthday gifts or it can drive a person or an entire people to desperation.'

We say to our friends: 'Wait, it will happen, you are still young.' But for many of my friends in the inner city and millions of the poor of this world, this is not the nature of their waiting. Indeed, if I were to choose one word to highlight the experience of the powerless at its deepest level of desperation, it is their waiting. They are subjected to the psychological violence of waiting. And waiting for what? In the long run, a radical change of values and priorities in the lives of those who have benefited (either by design or chance) from the institutions and the lifestyles created by those institutions which have cornered the access to the resources.

It is this kind of waiting which I find painful to watch in the lives of those with whom I exist. They wait for the dole; they wait for the hint of employment; they wait for a supplementary benefit; they wait for a sector of society to really live up to the philosophy of equal opportunities; they wait for the bureaucratic system to check its files; they wait for a white racist society to admit its own spiritual paralysis which prevents it facing up to itself with honesty.

A society which forces people to wait, either by way of its privileged classes or its bureaucratic system or a combination of both, is a society which has chosen the path of oppressor. 'Wait till we get inflation or our balance of payments right, then we will give realistic thought to those who are crying for a minimal human existence', is the articulation of a society which is suffering from spiritual bankruptcy. The truly noble society does not work towards a secure political and economic philosophy in which the plight of the poor will be given consideration; the truly noble society begins its thinking and planning from the position of those who are most in need. Positive discrimination is a logical rider to the Christian vision of life.

I went on a march in protest against these words, which were published in a public journal, by Lord Scarman:

> Policemen in general, and detectives in particular, are not racialist, despite what many black groups believe. Like any individual who deals with a vast cross-section of society, they tend to recognise that good and evil exist, irrespective of colour or creed. Yet they are the first to define the problem of the half-castes in Liverpool. Many are the products of liaisons

THE REALITIES OF A NEW COMMUNITY

between black seamen and white prostitutes in Liverpool 8, the red-light district. Naturally they do not grow up with any kind of recognisable home life.

Those words contain a violence besides which the physical violence on our milk-bottle-bombed streets pales into insignificance. I am on delicate ground here. In no way do I condone violence, encourage or wish to exist with violence. But one cannot discuss the question of violence morally by simply looking at the acts of violence. The morality of violence must be constructed from the causes which bring any person or group of people to a point of physical violence.

The words were an appalling insult to many of my friends in this area. I am not all that keen on marches—perhaps I am somewhat of a coward. But I went. A strange memory remains with me about that march. It was the security I felt when we arrived back in our own area. The cold stares, indeed the angry stares, of people in the centre of the town suddenly gave way to greetings from people in the area. I felt I had come home. There was a sense in which that march on one Saturday morning in one inner city, gathered together all our Saturdays and all our Inner Cities and shouted out, 'We are all equal and no man will stigmatise us. Creation is ours.' There was the rumour of human beings reaching for infinity. Negatively, I knew then, as I do now, there had to be a long vigil. It was the vigil which waited upon the agreement of many of us to review our values and priorities in our western world. As Peter Townsend put it, answering one of his critics:

PASSION FOR THE INNER CITY

On the basis of the national evidence, I would reject his view that 'poverty no longer conforms to a picture of Dickensian destitution, with the pauper in a pitiable state', and elsewhere in his article, 'that the poor are not outcasts'.

This is fundamentally to misperceive the relativity of the condition of poor people. They are living in the society of the 1980's rather than that of 1840-1870; and in this context the conditions of some at least are as bad, or worse, than those which Dickens observed more than 100 years ago.[2]

The economic, social, political and racial criteria which we invoke in this country are not the creation of the economically poor, the politically powerless, the socially unacceptable or the racially stigmatised. They are the the creation of all of us who refuse to base our anxiety for a worthy vision of life on those who are forced to wait, and often wait, with total hopelessness, for the right to creative work, power over destiny, a social welcome and the day when the colour of one's skin does not lead to stigmatisation.

In the long run I believe that this implies a waiting until certain sectors of society, having thrown away their myopic dependencies, will agree to be disturbed spiritually at some depth. As David Donnison has recently put it:

It grows clearer each day that the promise of minimal government which aims only to protect our property, reduce our taxes and disturb us as little as possible is a delusion. Whether in Labour or Conservative forms, it is leading to economic disaster, rising unemployment and violence in the streets.

THE REALITIES OF A NEW COMMUNITY

In the refusal to be disturbed is the seed, at least, of terrible sinfulness. If I universalise Christ to such an extent that everyone can rest comfortably with Him and His teaching, then the essential aspect of Christ's confrontation with false values is lost, or at least debased. 'It is not hard to stay alive', says Common Man at the end of *A Man for all Seasons*, 'just don't make trouble. And if you do make trouble make sure it is the kind of trouble they expect from you.'

The powerless of society are not what I should arrive at, having constructed a theology. They should be the amalgam of the experience since they are the victims of so much sinfulness, from which I begin constructing a theology. In my area, Churches came under fire because of a grant to a post-riot committee; I believe this was a sign for Christian hopefulness, not Christian anxiety.*

Far too often, the Christian community believes that its vocation to be a sign of contradiction means to contradict those who would be at enmity with the Church. It must also face up bravely to the fact that there will be division in its own midst. Therefore it will turn out to be a sign of contradiction to itself. When Christian leadership begins to allow itself to be governed by opinion polls alone, especially

---

* If it was an ambiguous situation, one should take comfort in the fact that the very word of God, especially in the voices of the prophets and of Jesus, is not without its ambiguities. If it were, the scandal of the Cross would never have emerged as a puzzling purpose of the mission of Christ, or better a stopping place on the way to Resurrection. One cannot get away from the fact that his lifestyle had a lot to do with him getting himself murdered.

PASSION FOR THE INNER CITY

in matters of standing on the side of the powerless of this world, its mission has run out of divine energy.

The Church can always take a leaf out of the book of the prophets of old when it defines its vocation. For they did not merely say there was a lot of idol worshipping around; they named both the idols and the worshippers. I suppose the urgent thing is that, if there should be days of signs of contradictions and seasons of division, they are about worthwhile matters, which are at the heart of God's ever unfolding process of a new creation. I believe these worthwhile matters often sink to bedrock in an ocean brought to a rather silly storm by the winds and the waves of ecclesiastical minutiae. And I believe this is where, not without some measure of guilt, I find my boredom, puzzlement and sense of ennui.

I must be careful here. There have been too many critical canvases painted, dominated by the forbidding and repelling tints of despair. Far too many of us keep on looking back in anger, and the looking back seems to cloud the possible perception of a hopeful future, or even paralyses present existence and action. There has been far too little sensitivity and, in a very superficial way, a carelessness in the presence of history. At the same time, though twenty years ago a new era of radical renewal did dawn, too many fears, too much entrenchment, and too persistent battles about past positions continue to occupy our minds. The structures and the very consciousness of the Christian community seems still to be weighed down by past securities and outmoded dependencies.

THE REALITIES OF A NEW COMMUNITY

The cry of the poor is a summons to change our lives radically

My concern is, as I look with love and care at the Christian community in which I have found, and continue to find, so much fulfilment in life, that I see a tendency to reform or renew by way of permutation. Let me attempt a very simple example here from Religious life. In doing so, I must repeat my realisation that structures must exist. But there are still present in religious life debates about the kind of government which that form of life needs today. When this question is asked, it tapers off into a debate about how many consultors a general or provincial should have; what will be the name of a local superior or does the title superior go altogether; how will the government maintain its overall authority at differing levels of religious life?

It seems to me that such questions constantly fail to face the very nature of government in religious life towards the close of the twentieth century. The 'experience of being ruled' has been questioned in its very nature by contemporary humanity. I believe it is being questioned because the democratic dream has exploded; there is disillusionment with leadership at all levels of human existence, for we have simply failed to live up to the boast to create a truly equal society. If I hold that this state of affairs, this malaise, is the experience only of secular society, then I fail to grasp the fact that patterns of secular government have a deep impact upon Christian government in terms of Church and the groupings which are an integral part of the Church like Religious life. But there is something more

141

to the present struggle of society. It is of a positive nature. Humanity, in the midst of its disillusionment, is invoking once again the very primitive experience of basic communal living.

What I am really questioning is the tendency to move things around to discover something new, or even to renew what is there. I believe that one has to search deeper to discover new urges which emerge from the spirit of humanity. Community, as a reality and an experience, is being expressed in all kinds of different ways. The Christian church has named itself a community—this was a key notion in the attempts of Vatican II to rewrite theology. If this is true, one cannot simply accept certain inherited structures and shape them more to the pattern of authentic community. The parish is a perfect example of this. Can the sociological unit of the parish, as we know it today, ever project the ideal of community? It cannot, if one simply takes the parish and renames it a community. One must ask many questions about 'the people' and of 'the people'. If it is really to respond to the definition of community, then there must be a sense of shared power over destiny.

If this is so, then the word of the pew must carry as much weight as the word of the pulpit. Both words must be brought together to search for the Word of God in life. This is not to demolish distinctive responsibilities and functions; it is not to phase out the reality of Christian teaching and doctrine, but it is to ask that Christian doctrine be worked out in its daily application in a dialogue and a dialectic based upon the fundamental unity in the Spirit of Jesus, not to mention the radical equality in the same Spirit.

THE REALITIES OF A NEW COMMUNITY

Nobody would suggest that this is an easy process, but at the heart of Faith is the call to and experience of search. The word of the pew is the articulation of many hopes, many insights and many anxieties. In my own area, the expression of Faith of the Christian community, the parish, must find its roots in the basic experience of the area. An inner city area cannot ignore its environment; it cannot fail to keep in mind the experience of so many broken promises; it cannot close its eyes to its racism; it cannot turn a blind eye to the fact that there is a vast hopelessness. On the other side of the coin, neither can it fail to contemplate all the goodness, all the resilience, all the continuing infinite reaching, all the buried wonder in the heart of a people which remains alive and well against all the odds. I cannot celebrate a true Eucharist—the most vital event of the Christian community—unless I understand and assimilate as far as possible, the pain of the waiting and the anger of those who have been stigmatised in so many different kinds of ways. I cannot ignore the many who, without any religious faith, have struggled for the liberation of the powerless. Thirsting and hungering after justice is not by any means the preserve of the Christian.

If old structures need to go to make such an experience more real and vital, then go they must. I can only take hold of existence when I face up to the need for death. Rising is paradoxically dependent upon dying. I must search for,or perhaps simply let in, the new dependencies which are hammering on the door of my timid and fearful soul. I must believe that these interwoven dependencies in human life will lead me to a rediscovery of the Christian demand, 'Be

PASSION FOR THE INNER CITY

dependent upon God'; lose yourself; die to yourself; rise and follow anew; 'Come and see'.

I make no secret of my own reluctance to face up to such a demand, for I believe such a demand entails a certain purification. It demands what is central to the philosophy and theology of the Congregation which has given me my life. I speak, obviously, of an attempt to understand and live the suffering of Christ. I am conscious, as surely every Christian is conscious, of the God revealed to me, the God of relationships. The triune God has not merely consecrated the notion of personhood; the triune God has consecrated the interaction of persons, the experience of relationships—and what is more important still, that experience has been consecrated as an experience of equality. My passion for knowledge, for love and for the poor of this world cannot be realised unless I am ready 'to exist with and suffer with' the poor of this world. This is only realised through the wonder, the pain and the enrichment of a mutual shared power over life. Only in this way am I to find my way through the darkness of my selfish forest into the clearing of community.

If I say that the inner city has brought me face-to-face, in a new way, with the meaning of the Trinity and the suffering of Jesus to reveal that Trinity, it has done so because the powerless, the poor of this world, are no longer a statistic. Religious poverty has had to be translated into the struggle of poor men and women. But I would go further and say that there can be no such things as a vital Church until this is the base from which all Christian faith begins in all Christian people. If this is ignored, we hurry from the horror

THE REALITIES OF A NEW COMMUNITY

of sinfulness, but also from something more positive: we hurry from a moment of God's inviting grace.

At no point in these pages have I turned with any kind of savage criticism upon my brother priests and religious, sisters and brothers. I dare not do so. For I am no different than they. Indeed so many of them remain a daily enrichment for my life. But our western Church has a long road ahead of it. Being 'poor in spirit' is agreeing to let go of all superficial dependencies for the sake of the development of the Kingdom of God. Poor in spirit means that I am ready to commit myself—no matter what the price, personal or communal—to the values of truth, justice, peace and goodness. Such commitment must mean a new and creative era for new ministries to arise; for a new disposition of power within the Christian community to emerge; new definitions must be found to express the deepest realities of the Church; leadership at all levels must ask itself how to create the context for charism to be let loose for the benefit of the Church and the world; rationalisation must give way more and more to the straight commitment to sacrifice; all false dependencies will need to be looked at in depth; I believe that it is in the cry of the poor that such a passion for renewal can begin.

The cry of the poor in our times is not merely a summons into new activity, it is a demand that we change our very lives radically. In our era, I do not believe that we can come to understand the meaning of the knowledge of God and creation, the love of God and creation, the celebration of God and creation, unless we agree to hear in the depths of our hearts the cry of the oppressed—a hearing which will

PASSION FOR THE INNER CITY

call each one of us, in all differing ways, 'to exist with and suffer with' the powerless. If we do not, and do not do so with some urgency, we shall betray the wonder of God's creation.

I believe I must always remain humble when facing history. I have a deep respect, not only for history in general, but also for the history of institutions. History may well be riddled with the sinfulness of humanity, but at the same time it is the process also of the creativity of God. Yet we humans make history. Making history is the expression of our innate freedom; but in making it, we can place so many layers over the wonder of human existence in which God is revealed. Too often, we build institutions, or we fight for institutions, to put off the inescapable need to grasp death in order to live again.

In such a world, 'having' has been so elevated that 'being' must struggle to survive. A qualitative world has had to give way to a quantitative one. Such remarks may appear as no more than the utterance of truisms. I would prefer to see them as the expression of the most basic qualities of human life. Perhaps they are even the articulation of the wonder of human existence. Certainly they are for me the only articulation of a nature upon which grace can build.

One night, in my own home, a young person became frighteningly violent in a physical way. When he calmed down, he came and sat on the end of the bed in my room and began to cry. Through the crying, he said that he had been pushed around and thrown out of institution after institution since he was four years of age. As I

THE REALITIES OF A NEW COMMUNITY

looked at him, sitting there with head bent and sobbing, I remembered a painting in one of the Passionist houses. It was a painting depicting the mockery of Christ in the hours of his suffering. The head was bent, the mocking cloak of royalty was slipping away from his shoulder, there were tears on his face and he sat on the edge of a broken pillar. It was not the physical suffering which made its impact on me and remained with me; it was the encompassing loneliness which projected itself and made an impact. As I looked at that young person, that was all I could see. I mumbled sympathetically and attempted to point to a future.

An isolated and exaggerated example? Perhaps. At the same time, I have looked into the eyes of too many human beings in the inner city only to see a tragic hopelessness. There can never be an authentic philosophy of equality of opportunity unless we face up to the urgent need to admit the charade we have all been part of, as we played the game of equality itself. For me as a Christian, priest, and religious— and I know I speak for many others in this regard—the institution of Christianity has been no exception to this process of conscious or unconscious oppression. We must be rid of it, no matter what the price we have to pay in terms of radical renewal.

If we do so, as Christians, we do no more and no less than accept the call to denial of self to answer the call of Christ. To follow Christ means to die to oneself. To reap a new harvest, or better to work towards a future in which those who are not yet born will reap a new harvest, demands the death of the seed, now. We are the seed, living to die in an era of history, dominated by what I have called the 'contrast experience' which makes a mockery of what it is to be all that is human.

I thank God for my Faith, for my priesthood and for my religious life. I thank God for so much historical richness and self-sacrifice that has gone into the making of my present. But I know that the superfluous layers of status, position, privilege and security must be stripped away to lay bare the power and the glory of being human and made new in the life, works, death and resurrection of Jesus Christ, Son of God and Son of Man.

Appendix: The priest-workers of France

I became an ordained priest during a stormy period in French church history: the time when the priest-worker movement in France came to an end. In fact, I was studying in Rome, ahead of my ordination, when the movement ended; I read the books, *France Pagan*, *Mission to the Poorest*, and *Priest Workman in Germany*; I vividly remember how they inspired and challenged me. They gave witness to the 'experience of existing with and suffering with'. It moved me deeply, and, though unspoken at that stage of life, it made me ask myself certain questions about priesthood and religious life in this country.

On 20th February 1954, a sad, yet historic meeting took place in the upstairs room of a café outside Paris. It was the Café de la Paix in the suburb of Villejuif. The multiplicity and complexity of causes which brought this meeting about do not immediately concern me here. Those who attended the meeting were involved not only in a process of decision-making impinging upon their own lives, but also in an exercise of critique which would affect the Church. It was a critical meeting which was to consider the future of the priest-worker movement in France.

Ten days later, each person at that meeting knew that if he had not left his job and resigned from his trade union, he

PASSION FOR THE INNER CITY

would find himself exposed to canonical sanctions which could gravely jeopardise his future ministry in the church. This was a personal crisis for each priest. But what were the implications of this meeting, indeed the whole movement, in terms of a critique, a challenge to the Church? This is a much deeper question.

In a recent article Julian Walter posed a number of questions relating the priest-worker movement to the English scene. I quote him at some length:

> The primary aim of priest-workers, as we have seen, is to evangelise a stratum in society which places more confidence in Marxism than in traditional Catholicism. Does such a stratum of society exist in Britain? Is there a class of people who have rejected Christianity in favour of another ideology? The Church has become pluralist, particularly in the sense that there is no longer an overriding 'Roman' pattern of Catholicism for all nations; each country develops its own pastoral style.

> French society is characterised by tensions between revolutions and absolutism, between clericalism and the 'esprit laic'. Do analogous tensions exist in Britain? Is the clergy exposed to the danger of losing the loyalty of one section of society, notably the underdogs, because it is too compromised in its relations with the political establishment? Would, for example, an English bishop be required to speak out on some special issue in terms as forthright as those used by Bishop Huyghe of Arras, when the priest-worker Hubert David was sacked in October 1970; 'There are two classes of men; those who are constantly begging for a job which they may lose at any time, and those who possess the absolute power to sack their employees'.

APPENDIX: THE PRIEST-WORKERS OF FRANCE

Finally there is the question of balance in the notion of the priesthood. As we have seen, the priest worker is more concerned with those who are outside the Church, than those who are within. Vatican II affirmed that the Church needs fishermen as well as shepherds. The relationship between them is sometimes tricky—in France as elsewhere. In France it is constantly affirmed that the Church's primary commitment is to the mission. Is this the case, or should it be the case, in Britain too ...?[1]

I believe Fr Walter is correct in drawing a distinction between England and France as he does. His words, however, were written in 1979, and I suspect many things may yet challenge the church as to where, exactly, it stands: the increased state of the poverty trap; the problems of mounting racism; the development of a new hard-right-wing politically, not to mention the predictable development of a new left; the appalling problem of the inner city.

Indeed, the Pastoral Congress of 1980 in Liverpool spoke fairly strongly to the hierarchy about its responsibilities to offer a critique of society, and to illuminate and empower the church in its mission for greater justice in Britain. That congress did not talk in generalities. It stated, for example, that it believed that membership of the National Front was incompatible with membership of the Christian community.

When some of my Passionist French priest worker confrères entered into a dialogue with us here in Liverpool, there were differences to be acknowledged, but there was also a fundamental base of agreement. It was an agreement which one does not always share with fellow religious and priests (not to mention laity!) in this country. This was the shared conviction that one can only minister in a situation of practical human suffering. This sharing, further, was not to be based upon theories mutually subscribed to. In fact I believe that the bridge between us was the conviction of the need to exist with and suffer with the people. The difference rested between our involvement in the broader world of community development, compared to their commitment to an industrial and worker milieu.

The desire for a church 'existing with and suffering with' was at the root of the early French priest-worker movement. Père Chenu, who was closely associated with the movement at the time of its condemnation, made this point to me very clearly. I think it has been one of the greatest sadnesses in recent church history that this fact has been all too often overlooked. If I may return to a traditional term already used, the movement led inevitably to an ascetic of life.

A Church in a state of alienation from the people in this country will never be defined on the level of dogma and doctrine. It rests upon something much deeper, something which belongs to the 'order of existence'. In spite of much reflection and action in recent years in the church—even after Vatican II—those books are as relevant as ever. They are relevant in their spiritual challenge. I quote here some of the passages which both inspired and troubled me over twenty- five years ago. I hope they will help now to tease out some of the elements which are part of the answers to the questions I have put to myself, for they are a graphic, not to say dramatic, underlining of the meaning of 'existing and suffering with'. Just in case anyone thinks we have come a long way in recent years spiritually, I would tentatively suggest that Loew, Perrin, Godin and the rest came a long way nearly forty years ago and even suffered for it.

I would ask the reader to read each of these quotations with care and with openness. My own comments will come at the end of the series of quotations. I do this not merely for the sake of allowing the content of thought to come through clearly and in an uninterrupted fashion. No, it is much more than that. I would like these words to be approached in a meditative way.

The cycle of Christian predictability

From 'France Pagan?' by Maisie Ward

We have now reached the very heart of the problem. We are in front of that brick wall against which we have, one after another during the last ten years, hurled ourselves in vain. We find a new road which seems to us promising— and behold at the end of it the wall is there again. Let us look at a recent instance.

Everyone has heard of Father Lhande and his grand and noble campaign in the suburbs of Paris, of the enthusiasm it aroused, the splendid devotion expended, the vocations to which it gave birth. Superhuman efforts were made to bring Christianity to this mass of proletarians: a hundred churches built by the Cardinal's workshops, new parishes, the blossoming of various good works. All France was applauding, all France full of hope.

Let us sum up the results. From one point of view magnificent, for a single soul is worth a lifetime of work and many hundreds of souls were converted, but as for penetrating the proletarian world, the effect was nil. A hundred new Christian communities were founded, but what did they accomplish? Out of the pagan world they gathered a few hundred Christians who had fallen into it or who had been afraid to practise their religion in it. A few dozen more or less hostile families were won over from the pagan and brought into the parochial world. Good works were started which there, as elsewhere, skimmed the cream of human values among the young, succeeding in holding some few of them. And today have not these parishes really become close corporations just like the rest?

Often founded and managed by saints, they are fervent sources of Christian life, but without expansion. At first their zealous founder often went fishing in proletarian waters. Then the disciples they gained merged with the parish, the proletarian world was left again to its fate.

How painful, how impossible for us to depict here the drama of many priestly souls who had hoped for something else had wholly devoted themselves... some still hope on, struggle on-and run against the old high wall. Most of them change their aim and begin to look for quality rather than quantity. Does not, they ask, the love of one fervent soul make up to Christ for many pagans? And they begin to work for an elite.

Is then the proletariat accursed? These little ones, the humble, the poor—no one seems to want them. All of us are rich—if not with money, yet with the wealth Of being respected, of having good connections (which, at a time of scarcity and restrictions, is worth even more than money), with the wealth, too, of culture and traditions. And we are only too much inclined to forget the poor who lack all these things.

Christ preferred the poor.

APPENDIX: THE PRIEST-WORKERS OF FRANCE

There is one fact in the Church's history which should lead us to reflect deeply. The Church's members have their share of human defects and Christ is ever watching to bring back his Spirit, whom the Christians are forever losing. Under the impulse of the Spirit they think much of the poor and the little ones and they found institutions to care for them. But, after a few generations, these institutions, these societies are working for less destitute people, the change is often marked.

How many societies founded to help prisoners are now doing something quite different?

How many teaching orders that are today instructing well-to-do girls were founded to teach the poor?

How many societies founded to work in public hospitals end up by opening nursing homes?...

A founder picks up little street boys and his spiritual sons conduct professional schools to which the pupils do not come from the level of the populace.

An Order is founded for the poor of the countryside; it goes into cities and takes on other kinds of work.

Scouting is started for street-boys and is quickly turned into the preserve of the better-off.

We are setting this down, without bitterness, but simply as illustrating a law that runs through all human activities.

What follows? Are the little ones, the poor, the humble the proletarians always to be sacrificed, in spite of Christ's preference for them?

Or must we not rather tirelessly and endlessly strive for a basic renewal in the evangelising of the people? Never must so vast a human world be left ignorant and abandoned.[2]

Breaking the cycle with existence

From 'Mission to the Poorest' by M.R. Loew

Opposite is the family to whom I shall live in the closest possible proximity for two years; one room as usual doing duty for a whole house, lavatory included. The family consists of a grandfather, a grandmother, and a little girl of twelve... Good morning, good evening—our relations scarcely go beyond that. One day, about twelve, Madame Antoine, having just made a fine fish noodle soup, sends me in a plate by her little girl. Some weeks later, I become her boarder; a little later still, we are all four living together, having our two rooms in common.

It is only then that, a little by little as when a mist begins to thin, the true countenance and the deep personal life of the Antoine family is revealed to me...

But this is still only a surface view of the Antoine family. At the end of six months I am thoroughly familiar with the customs of the old couple, their little fads, their joys and their grouses...

I am truly part of the district, although I often leave it at six or seven in the morning and only return late in the evening) since I am still busying myself in the town on economic and social questions. But the fact of sleeping there, of being in the true and juridical sense of the word domiciled in the district) makes my position enormously different from what it would be if I spent the whole day working in the district but disappeared every night to go and sleep at the monastery The first and most important effect of this nightly habitat is that it precludes any kind of hypocrisy. We really do share the same

APPENDIX: THE PRIEST-WORKERS OF FRANCE

life because we suffer the same difficulties, the same troubles, and drink the same wine, often from the same glass. And this is where the real social and religious problems are to be met— not in complicated theological abstractions, but in the simple questions devolving on lice and such things.[3]

In the cycle but not of it

From 'Mission to the Poorest' by M.R. Loew

Tell me quite honestly—if, on your way, you had recognised your mother or your sister, would you have offered her to the curious gaze of the public? Would you have found it in you to publish her name, this woman or that child we have both tried to help?

I do not believe that you have the right to violate the secrets of their lives, of their physical, moral, social wretchedness. They are not curiosities, the subjects of an experiment, something to be exposed in showcases or popular magazines.

Father, you have never wept with hunger, you have never known what it is like to be really out of work, to hear someone say, 'Give me your name. You will be notified.'

I entreat you, respect the secrets of others, do not disclose things which are not yours to tell.[4]

The call for articulation in suffering

From 'Mission to the Poorest' by M.R. Loew

One hesitates long after such burning words. Silence, is not this the safest course? There are decencies more compelling, a nakedness more distressing, than those of the body.

And yet how is one to act effectively, to avoid betraying the truth, if one does not enlighten those who are unaware of what is actually happening barely a few hundred yards from where they live? How, without shouting at the top of one's voice, can one prevent the distance widening, the gulf deepening every day between those who could act - who must act—but who are unconscious of the situation, and those who can no longer do anything!..

This is no matter of trying to touch people's feelings, appealing to their compassion; rather it is one of crying out before it is too late, before the day when we shall hear it from his own lips, the words of Christ: 'As long as you did it not to one of the least of these...'

We should be but part witnesses of Christ if we b witness to Jesus of Nazareth only; we also have to proclaim the sufferings of the body of Jesus as it exists at the present time, as we encounter it every day in our cities, wandering vagrant, lacking shelter, lacking air and light and warmth alone in the world without work, without hope and without God... Your secret, my destitute brothers, my companions whom I love and respect with all that is best in me, does not belong to yourselves alone. It is that of the Saviour, just as your body is not yours alone but His too. And we all communicate in this same body ... we too although after you.

APPENDIX: THE PRIEST-WORKERS OF FRANCE

In short, we are but one.

And since again the remedy for our ills is not found in the chemists' shops or laboratories but consists in changing the social pressure, it is imperative that all cooperate in the immense effort of recovery.

Millions of men have fallen to the bottom of the abyss, and who can flatter himself that he is far from the edge.

This book, among so many others, sends an appeal to all Christians of good will for a gigantic heave at the rescue line— gigantic, yes, and yet in practice it is so simple; for all one has to do is to take one's place at the rope.[5]

Organisation and action

From 'Mission to the Poorest' by M.R. Loew

The Residence is not a game or record of visits, of advice, of surgical dressings and injections. Love and physical strength are not enough to give without the effort of the mind. The Residence is not there merely to fight day by day against the physical and moral sufferings of an area. It is there to take part in the great movements of man's civilisation, especially in the worker movement.[6]

Is the appeal to history irrelevant?

Many friends have questioned, and with justification, my appeal to the priest-worker movement of the 1940s and 1950s. Indeed, during a consultation in Paris with a theologian who was intimately concerned in that movement, I learned that he considered this appeal to the past virtually meaningless.

I have already alluded to the fact that this movement meant something to me on a personal level; and these pages are in the nature of a personal reflection. But it is not mere personal admiration which moves me to return to the priest-workers. There is something much deeper. And that something which is much deeper is at the same time bound up with the central ideas of these pages.

Close on twenty years ago the Church set out on a path of what was then called aggiornamento, or coming up to date. An era of renewal and reform was announced. The popular image of the era was summed up in the words of Pope John XXIII: 'open the windows and let the fresh air in.' A series of magnificent and profound documents came from the major event of those days, the Second Vatican Council.

That Council believed to be so profound in the life of the Church that we spoke of it starting a new age in the Church, 'the post-Vatican II era'. No one would dare minimise the Council's historic importance. One major theme running through the whole conciliar reflection was the unique importance of the story of mankind itself: that is to say, the Council recognised the fact that that the actual and lived-

APPENDIX: THE PRIEST-WORKERS OF FRANCE

out history of humanity was essential to its conclusions. One quotation will suffice to make the point:

> Just as it is in the world's interest to acknowledge the Church as a social reality and a driving force, so too the Church is not unaware how much it has profited from the history and development of mankind.[7]

But a question must be asked about the Vatican Council's intention. Is this 'history of mankind' merely a reference point which the Church must take into account for its own development and mission? Or is it, much more profoundly, a necessary source for all theology, speculative as well as practical? I would be willing to accept that the latter, deeper understanding was in the Council's mind—was, perhaps, a principal motivation for many of the members of the Council. But I offer it as my opinion that the first and narrower interpretation in fact articulates the real underlying theological view of the Council. To put it another way: for the Council, discerning the word and action of God in history meant primarily examining the life, thought and action of the Church, and only secondarily the life, thought and action of mankind.

This judgement is, I think, supported by the fact that the documents of Vatican II have now acquired the role of an older, 'manuals' theological approach to the life of the Church. It is as if it were more important that consciousness and structure in the Church should be subjected to change through introspective reflection rather than through reflection upon the movement and stirrings of the human spirit. Pius XII once spoke about taking the Church out of the sacristy. But, I am suggesting, the sacristy continues to have more influence than the street on the life of the Church: Vatican II, wonderful though it was, was inspired more by the former than by the latter.

For all these reasons, the priest-worker movement seemed, and still seems, to me of greater importance on one level than Vatican II. It contains the practical formulation of a theological principle, recognised to a degree by Vatican II, but not worked out to its final conclusion. I do not, of course, suggest that the priest-worker movement itself succeeded in working out this principle fully or satisfactorily—that could hardly have been expected of a movement of thirty years ago. But it did bring the Christian consciousness to an awareness of the alienation of Church and working world, and it did explore deep into the experience of the working world to find a source for theological reflection and development. Above all, I think, it highlighted how a new asceticism was a sine qua non for the future life of the Church.

My extended quotations from the priest-worker experience and epoch have, I hope, established these points. The first quotation—'The Cycle of Christian Predictability', as I have called it—traces the cyclic process which eventually mars so much initially enterprising thought and action—and shows how all too often this can be due to the intervention of middle-class attitudes and culture where they are inappropriate. The third quotation, 'In the Cycle but not of it', points out just how much sensitivity is demanded in a missionary endeavour which authentically attempts to initiate change in the world of the body and

APPENDIX: THE PRIEST-WORKERS OF FRANCE

the spirit. The fourth and fifth quotations, 'The Call for Articulation in Suffering' and 'Organisation and Action', lead us to see how solidarity in life and organisation in action are crucial to any real development.

But it is the second quotation—'Breaking the Cycle'—which is the necessary link. It is the link which, for me, expressed most fully the theology of 'existence with and suffering with'—the need for awareness, openness, sensitivity, compassion. All five emphasize the context of industry and labour, and I hope I may be able to establish my own credentials in that respect. But the essential point is this: it is human experience which is the necessary starting-point—a starting-point not merely to be examined, analysed, and acted upon, but a starting-point to be 'existed with and suffered with'.

Bibliography

Chapter 1

1 Jacques Maritain, *The Range of Reason*, London 1953, 121f.

Chapter 2

1 Fr Congar, *Concilium V*, 2 (May 1966), 28-39.
2 Bertrand Russell, *Autobiography*, 9.
3 Karl Rahner, *Theological Investigations VIII*, 169
4 M.R. Loew, *Mission to the Poorest*, 75f.

Chapter 3

1 David Knowles, *Bare Ruined Choirs*, Cambridge 1959, 24.
2 R.W. Southern, *Western Society and the Church in the Middle Ages*, Harmondsworth 1970,256.
3 L. Little, *Religious Poverty and the Profit Economy in Medieval Europe*, London 1978, 217.

Chapter 4

1 Thomas Merton, *The Monastic Journey*, London 1977, 170.
2 ibid., 171
3 ibid., 171f.
4 Jacques Maritain, *The Range of Reason*, 121.
5 M.R. Loew, *Mission to the Poorest*, London 1950, 37ff.

Chapter 5

1 R.W. Southern, *Western Society and the Church in the Middle Ages*, Harmondsworth 1970, 330.

2 ibid.

3 ibid., 339.

4 ibid., 344f.

5 Presumably a reference to Raymond Hostie, *Religion and the Psychology of Jung*, Sheed & Ward 1957.

6 David Knowles, *Christian Monasticism*, 53.

7 ibid.

8 Karl Rahner, *Notes on a Journey*, The Month.

9 Edward Schillebeeckx, *The Christ*, London 1980, 738.

10 ibid.

11 James H. Cone, *God of the Oppressed*, New York 1975, 44.

Chapter 6

1 Jacques Maritain, *True Humanism*, London 1938, xii.

2 ibid., xif.

3 Gabriel Marcel, *The Philosophy of Existence*, London 1948, 2.

4 Gabriel Marcel, *The Mystery of Being I*, London 1950, 2.

5 Pope Paul VI, as quoted in *The Tablet*, August 1979.

Chapter 7

1 Martin Buber, *Between Man and God*, London 1969, 33.

Chapter 8

1 M.R. Loew, *Mission to the Poorest*, 40.

2 Peter Townsend, *Poverty in the United Kingdom*, Harmondsworth 1979, 917,921.

3 ibid., 921f.

4 Barbara Ward, *The Home of Man,* New York 1976, 3f.

5 ibid., 10 (emphasis added).

6 Elaine Morgan, *Falling Apart*, London 1978, 140.

7 Dr Little, *Religious Poverty and the Profit Economy in Medieval Europe*, 213.

8 ibid., 214.

9 T.L. Blair, *The International Urban Crisis*, London 1974, 117.

10 RW Southern, *Western Society and the Church in the Middle Ages*, Harmondsworth 1970, 274f.

11 Stanislaus Breton, from *The Passionist VII,* 1979, 77.

Chapter 9

1 Bertrand Russell, *Autobiography,* 161.

2 Jack Dominian, *Proposals for a New Sexual Ethic*, London 1977, 68.

Chapter 10

1 Brian Wicker, *Culture and Liturgy*, London 1963, 151.

2 Peter Townsend, in *New Society*, 17 September 1981, 478.

Appendix

1 Fr Julian Walter, *The Month*, London.

2 Maisie Ward, *France Pagan?*, London 1949, 107ff.

3 M.R. Loew, *Mission to the Poorest*, London 1950, 37ff.

4 ibid., 19.

5 ibid., 19f.

6 ibid., 18.

7 Eileen Burke-Sullivan et. al, *The Church in the Modern World*, 44.

Lightning Source UK Ltd.
Milton Keynes UK
UKHW040754100222
398459UK00002B/254